Lexèywa

~

I Pass the Torch to You

Beatrice Elaine Silver

electromagneticprint

Front cover, *"The TRC"* and back cover *"The Cafeteria"*
artwork and interior images reproduced with permission
by Robert Bateman Secondary School, Art Activism program;
and the Abbotsford School District, British Columbia.

www.electromagneticprint.com

"The Indian Affairs Nurse"

For my mother Jean Silver, a Survivor,
and for my sisters and brothers who are also Survivors.

And for all Indian Residential School Survivors,
their descendants, and for those who died in the schools
or tragically died after leaving, from complications
associated with Indian Residential School.

Contents

Chapter One

My Dream - A Nightmare

"First Arrival"

I was falling, falling, falling! I awoke with a start. It was dark – pitch dark – and smelled of a dilapidated dank old house. Still half asleep, I tried to see around me: there were little iron beds with tiny mounds under blankets. I thought, this isn't home, no mom and dad here, no little brother! Where is my mom and everyone? This is not our bedroom, not our house!

Then it hit me like a smack and my heart fell. I realized I was in the cold, stark dorm in the Residential School called St. Mary's, not sure where it was exactly, but somewhere far from my mom. Well, I thought determinedly, I'm going to find my big sisters Mona, Dianna, and Frieda; they're here, I know they are.

I jumped out of that cold, starchy, unfamiliar bed and took off for the door. The old hallway was smelly and narrow. The pale green paint showed in the dim light. I ran down that hallway to the end. I ran into the door and grabbed the handle; I started pulling and pushing, it was locked! I cried out, "Mona!" No answer. I cried out again and again, "Mona!! Jake!! Frieda!!" There was no sound but a hollow echo, my echo.

I screamed and cried out for my big sisters but nothing happened and no one came. Soon I was screaming louder, and louder! I ran back and forth across the green hallway, banging on the two heavy green doors and the cold ugly walls, desperate to find my sisters. They had separated us immediately when we arrived at the school the day before and I didn't even get to see them!

At that moment I suddenly remembered it all with a

shock. Still, I was desperately hoping I was only dreaming! I continued to cry and scream until I felt sick. I stayed there holding my stomach and wanting to throw up as I screamed, trying to wake somebody up. Anybody.

In the dark of night I could barely make out the shapes of the little girls back in the dormitory room behind me, who sleepily pushed their heads out from under the rough, uncomfortable blankets. They looked at me mournfully and then shivered and just went back under their covers.

I went to the brightly lit bathroom. There was a frightened little girl wrapped in a rough army blanket. I asked her, "Why are you sitting on the toilet like that?" I was shocked to find out that she had been sitting there all night. "The Sister put me here," she said. "Why?" I asked, unbelievingly; feeling horrified and sorry. "Because I peed my bed," she answered, and when she spoke she started crying quietly. I told her to come to bed but she replied that she could not or she would get strapped. I walked away in my own lost and tragic sadness, feeling hers too. I know now my little school mates were carrying their own sorrows, as if what they saw and heard and experienced there was too much for them to even try to give comfort to anyone else. The girls were awake but they remained silent. Only my incessant screaming and raging with frustration could be heard, and nobody came.

In exhaustion, I lay down on the little hard cot and cried quietly, rocking and choking on my sobs. Finally I gave in to a restless sleep. This was my first of many hopeless, lonely, sad nights in residential school.

Chapter Two

Where My Life Began In Kilgard

"Teacher"

I am Beatrice Elaine Silver from Sumas First Nation, which we called Kilgard, five miles east of Abbotsford, British Columbia. My parents were Ambrose and Jean Silver and they had eleven living children by the time I went to Indian Residential School in Mission. I am the youngest girl, or, as my mom said, "the baby girl." I have a younger brother who I grew up with for a little while, here and there – Norman Patrick – but my big brothers called him Ike. I had six brothers and four sisters. My oldest brother was Ray, then came Dave, Herman, Aleck and Lyle who were away working ever since I could remember. They began their own big families when I was very young. Then there were my sisters Yvonne, Frieda, Mona and Dianna and our "sister-cousins" – raised with me and my siblings – Rena and June. Our traditions were strong concerning our families: cousins were often raised together and treated as siblings. Thus, the huge families among our people are still common today.

As well, I discovered later that my parents lost some babies before I was born. There was Margaret and Peter, and some miscarriages. I especially remember hearing my Mom talk sadly and so quietly about their one son, a big brother whom I never knew: Dolton. When I was older, mom told me Dolton died in Port Alberni residential school when he was very young, twelve years old. She said the authorities didn't call her or dad about his death and nothing was told to them if he had been ill before he died. My oldest brother Ray told us that they were separated in school and rarely saw one another. He says one day he was put on the ferry and harshly informed that he was going home; he and Dolton.

He was happy about that but he couldn't find his brother

Dolton on the ferry. He asked the priest again, who reassured him Dolton was on the ferry. He still couldn't find Dolton so he kept asking, and finally the priest said, "Your brother is downstairs in a coffin." Dolton died mysteriously in that horrid school in Port Alberni, which was at least two hundred miles and a two hour ferry ride away from Kilgard. My brother Ray was thirteen. He told our parents he would not return to residential school; he just refused. He began working at thirteen years old. There began a new chapter in his life, helping our parents raise his sisters and brothers. I was born two years before his oldest child Louise. I knew my brother more like a father than a big brother. He treated me and my sisters so well, doing his best to help look after us after our father died when I was seven years old.

Our mother had an extremely difficult life doing her best to keep us fed and in clothes. Those were difficult times indeed but I would rather be at home than in that foreign and loathsome residential school that I later learned to survive in. Mom, Jean, was always soft spoken and gentle with Ike and me, giving us what she could as a parent. No matter the situation she exuberated unconditional love for her children. However, even as a child I could sometimes recognize a dark cloud underneath her mothering activities. I knew she was devastated about times past. Mom carried this sadness all her life as she did many other tragedies in her life, trying to hide it deep within. She mourned lost children, she cried apologetically when she could not give us things others received easily: pretty clothes, TV, movies, toys and treats in stores, and even basic necessities were often unattainable. All of that didn't matter to me, I had her. She didn't drink for years and my little brother and I were happy before residential school. We got our mother's complete attention as children. Although material things were very few it was having her that meant the most in my young life.

Our well-being came before hers. Our mother Jean could only cope with so much I'm sure, although she seemed to roll with whatever struck her, including physical abuse. Mom began drinking alcohol after all her children were taken away to residential school and our older brothers moved on to go logging, then to get married and raise their own children. She had us younger ones close with her always when we came home from school until my father died. After mom started drinking us younger ones lived with older siblings, during school breaks most often. I know now that her drinking was a bit of freedom my mother wanted to have after many years of sacrificing for all of us and enduring the tough challenging life made more difficult by the abuse put upon her all her married life. I continue to carry my mother's sorrow and pain which I saw within her, but I have long since been on my own healing journey and I will be until I go over to the better side to join her. I tell her still, "I will not cry anymore, I am healing mom," and I know she knows this. She always said she would watch over us when she died. I would always tell her, "You'll be with us forever mom." She would give us her special smile: funny, kind but secretive, and reply, "Yeah, I will be with you all – with all my kids."

"My kids were the only friends I had all those years," she would say softly. That still makes me sad today as I remember so much, so many times she could have used a few friends who were more than just little kids. My good childhood memories are laced with sadness. My family, especially mom, mourned brother Dolton's untimely death. My eldest brother Ray, who recently passed at 87 years old, always mentioned him sadly when he talked of our life long ago.

Today there remains that tragic mystery clouding over my brother Dolton's death. He himself is a heartbreaking mystery to me as he was born to my parents almost thirty years before me. A few pictures is all I have seen of him, and a few bits of information. He was a handsome blond little guy. My family sadly spoke proudly of their memories of him, sweet memories clearly laced with woe and helpless longing. There were many speculations but our family still does not know how our brother Dolton died there tragically, horribly.

Later at a healing event, I met an elderly gentleman who also went to school in Port Alberni. I had earlier listened to him tell horror stories of his residential school experiences in a major TV documentary. In the film, this man had reminisced about how he and another boy would be driven to a nearby house, often, where they were horrifically abused sexually and also subjected to further unbelievable acts of horror. I approached him when I saw him at an event and introduced myself, relating that I too am a residential school survivor. We talked like close friends, sharing all too familiar terrible experiences.

I told him of a brother I never had the pleasure of knowing, who mysteriously died in Port Alberni residential school. He listened compassionately with ears and eyes wide open. When my new friend realized I was speaking of Dolton and I was Dolton's little sister, he made a strangled, shocking noise in his language and held me tight. Emotional with tears, he could say no more. I knew then that a heinous crime was the cause of my brother's tragic death in that evil school. I believe the elder, now gone to the better side, knew and shared those horrors together with my brother. I can only imagine what this kind, elderly gentleman knew of the incident. This handsome compassionate elder was there with brother Dolton and most likely witnessed and experienced the unthinkable that no child should ever be aware of, much less be a part of.

I told very few people of this as it was too much to ponder and would only bring up more heartache for my family. I'm sure my Mom, dad and brothers suspected abuse and murder. It was not talked about until much later when as adults we tried to find out more of his death. There are no records of how my brother died at the tender age of twelve years old.

With unshed tears, as I reminisce, I realize now that my mother Jean also experienced abuse and tragedy. In Kuper Island Indian Residential School she had to endure her own horrible abuse as well as her dear sister's. She never spoke much of it. I know now there was so much sorrow that mom carried silently.

As I was the youngest, I was with her later when we all suffered the loss of two of her caring and generous adult sons, Aleck and Dave. Aleck was killed at age 33 in a logging accident, leaving five beautiful children and a loving pregnant wife Joan. I cry knowing their pretty baby girl Laurel never had the pleasure of knowing her kind quiet father. She holds stories that are told to her about her dad Aleck tucked in her heart, I'm sure, as those are the only stories she knows him by. Following those two tragedies, my brother Lyle was in a horrible car accident at 34 years old which altered his life totally, leaving only traces of the man he used to be. So Mom grieved for her living son too, as his life was hell for him physically, emotionally, mentally and spiritually until he passed over to the better side a few years ago.

In a little nutshell I can see now I was born into what people refer to as the intergenerational effects of colonization generally, and Indian Residential School in particular. My early life did not seem that way to me. My family loved me and I loved them; that is what was important to me as a child. Indeed our entire Nation suffered poverty and deprivation. Early reserve life was totally controlled by the Department of Indian Affairs: the almighty government. There was no other way to live. We were not allowed to leave the reservation. If anyone wanted to live off-reserve they had to enfranchise, give up all their rights as a native person – whatever those rights were worth then. The government dictated everything we could or could not do. Hunting and fishing were monitored so severely that food was scarce. My father trapped and fished only when the government said he could, which was not very often and tightly controlled.

I loved it when dad went out to the ridge to hunt ducks. Mom made delicious soup with dumplings and fried bread. Our old stove was only heated by firewood so she often collected wood to cook and keep us warm. In spite of the obvious hardships, I didn't actually realize at the time how hard they worked to provide us with food and comfort. Dad would go out with huge sacks and harvest wild hazelnuts in the Fall. Sometimes he took me and my little brother. Although they are covered with needles, hazelnuts are so delicious when dried and eaten in the cold Winter months!

At that time, during my tender years with my family in

Kilgard, my life was normal to me. I knew we didn't have everything we needed and we were very poor but it was my home and community. It was my life, my Kilgard Reserve that was my home that I loved. I was happy and safe there in my early years as long as my mother was there and my big sisters, when they were home from that mysterious place they disappeared to called "St. Mary's." I wondered what and where it was. Too soon I was to find out.

I take pride in being the second youngest in my family, the youngest girl with my little tiny brother whom my big brothers nicknamed Ike. They were great at giving nicknames, my sister Dianna was "Jake" because she is not to be messed with and she always stomped about in little red cowboy boots. When my big brothers were home they teasingly called me TSheh' (Scheh') because of my long hair that I didn't like brushed, especially not by my sister Dianna, anyway, at least I thought that was why they called me that. She brushed my hair often with impatience and pulled it back so tightly I was sure that's why people said I looked Japanese. I didn't know what Japanese was; I took it to be another mysterious woman who came down from the mountain to get us if we did not obey our parents. Of course now I know of Japanese culture and admire it greatly.

Anyway, TSheh' is the name my big brothers used to playfully call me, and I was not fond of it. This is the name of a scary mysterious spirit; one of mom's stories told to keep children a bit afraid of the dark, and therefore safe and in-doors at night.

By the time I remember life, or as my mom called it, "When

I came-to," my big brothers were off far away to work, logging in Alaska mostly. I remember being so happy when those big handsome men walked in carrying many boxes of yummy food and fruit and pocket change for Ike and me, money for mom and unfortunately a bottle for our dad. Mom would happily bustle about cooking up food for all and often their guy friends were with them, Tommy Kelly and the Francis boys to name a few. Heh! Most of the time they had beer, restless thoughts and only wanted to hurry away to do whatever young cool guys did after long months of isolated work.

I would hear mom telling them to stay out of trouble and not to fight with others – or each other – and especially not the RCMP, who they called bulls. I used to think the "bulls" must sure be big and dreadful creatures. Now some RCMP are family and friends whom we respect and love dearly.

My brothers taught us to defend ourselves when they came home. They taught us to box, as most of them boxed. Dave had "one more fight to become professional," I wold hear the adults say. The brothers who didn't go in the ring fought in other places, they could be quite rowdy, and they were referred to as The Silver Boys, with more than a little dread.

I wasn't a very good boxer as my gift seemed to be in debating, arguing and negotiating with my little friends and brother (who was easy to win over until he grew older). I used to play a lot with the few little kids on the reserve and close relatives that came to Kilgard, and I exercised my "leadership skills." I remember my cousin-brother Steven Point who I grew up with and how when we played he used to say, "I'm going to be the Prime Minister when I grow up!" I would reply with equal confidence and conviction, "I'm going to be the Store Keeper!" Because our store keeper was in charge of everybody in Kilgard, like the old Indian Agent Mr. Applebee – a very unwelcome character. I didn't like that but I liked the being-in-charge part. All the community's family allowances went to him and in turn he told you what you could or could not buy, and how much people owed him. He was not a revered boss at all in our community and our parents meekly obeyed him.

My thinking around becoming the store keeper was something along the lines of, "I can make things better; our families can have all they need and want, and all the kids can have lots of treats!" Well I later did more than that and so did Steven: he went on to become a judge and then Lieutenant Governor of British Columbia, and I went on to be a teacher and an owner of a gallery gift shop, among many other things, but that's another story.

Those days and times I remember fondly and sometimes sadly. My brothers and sisters all worked hard in their respected fields. My siblings raised good families in spite of the hardships they all experienced. I was and still am proud of them all. They each had a hand in raising me at various times in my life. I remember a lot of good things in my early childhood, however I have forgotten a lot also. I have forgotten many of the things that are too painful to remember. The residential school era is a difficult piece of our history for sure. The good times at home are mainly good memories. Times with my family were secure: even when tough situations arose, I had my family.

I think of times when excitement came into my life in my early childhood. I felt happy when new people came to our home and community. If I was lucky, one of the brothers would bring a pretty girl home. I liked that! To me it was exciting to see pretty ladies from other places: wearing high heels; swishing skirts; and adorned with dangly earrings which I admired profusely.

One pretty long-haired girl who came home with my brother wore the prettiest little beaded Indian girl earring I ever saw. It swung gracefully from her ear. I kept staring at her and her earring. She laughingly said she lost the other at the dance hall they called Delta Hall, or perhaps, he thought, at our house. Because I loved it she gently took it off her ear and clipped it onto mine. Well after that I was determined to find the missing earring! I loved beautiful things and when I was introduced to pretty earrings, I loved them too. Well Mom helped me search for the beaded Indian girl earring, but sadly we had no luck. What I did find during that search was the fact that I wanted to have pretty dangly earrings too.

My Mom had an idea. She let me go through all her colored buttons to make dangly earrings with. She would smile that funny smile as I threaded pretty buttons and hung them dangling right over my ears, swishing my hair about and thinking, "Now I'm as pretty as those fancy girls." My personality was coming forth as well as my character. If you desire good things in life, and there are obstacles and challenges to overcome, never let them make you give up on your goals. I learned well from my parents, sisters and brothers.

Herman and Lyle were the guys always in Alaska logging. Big brother Ray, Dave and Aleck worked closer to home. Ray worked in our Kilgard brick plant since he was fifteen, and Aleck logged just across the border in the United States most of the time. No matter where they were, they were still my big tough brothers and everyone knew not to mess with them. And not to mess with me either. Although they fought one another at times, heaven help anyone who attacked a brother! They protected each other. Some of them did the craziest things but they were always there for family.

I remember the time brother Herman unbelievably brought a tiny abandoned bear cub home from some logging camp. He brought him in to our house, unannounced, and boldly introduced him to our family. He and my dad made a home for him under our house. He was cute and very attached to Herman who taught that little cub to protect him and his possessions. My brother Ike and I were very little then.

Yes, there are many stories about Herman And The Bear. He began growing fast. My dad always got apples from our orchard for him. One day, Ike and I were in the bedroom with mom while she sewed clothes. We were getting noisy playing about, so mom told us "be quiet, remember the Bear under the house." Sure enough, she no more than said that and the Bear was standing in the bedroom doorway. Ike and I looked at him in fright as he watched us, standing still with his pigeon toes turned in, looking big and fierce. He watched us for a minute – which seemed an eternity – then he turned and sauntered off with a purpose, back downstairs to his house. He was only checking on us, we knew, because he protected our household. Mom silently kept sewing.

Herman was quite a character and was always doing something surprising which no longer surprised our family or community. I should mention that the bear grew so huge he had to be turned over to the wild animal authorities. I think my parents were happy about that. I think the entire community was happy about that.

As for the sisters, well... the brothers were very strict and very protective, even with their clothing and, later, my clothing. No tight clothes; no short skirts. My sisters were sure to dress nicely and modestly. Except for me. When I got old enough to be able to choose my own clothes, mini-skirts and go-go boots and the like were the rage. My sister Frieda bought me clothes that were in style despite my brothers' comments and warnings. I simply took off the other way and avoided them so my attire would not be inspected. Those mini-skirt teen years came right after residential school, thank The Creator!

When I was very young "The Silver Brothers," as they were often referred to, had big families. Ray and his wife Irene had eleven children: Louise, who is a bit younger than me, Janet, Kathy, Verna, Bernice Ray Jr., Ambrose, Janice, John, Edna and Paula. Herman, my devil-may-care brother, wasn't going to let Ray outdo him!... no way, he had twelve children with his wife Barbara: Herb, Janey, Audrey, Elaine, Charlotte, Vernon, (D), Jaqueline, Geraldina, Richard, Crystal, Jennette, Dianne and finally Deborah! My poor tired sisters in law Barbara and Irene! So many children and many of them were girls, pretty girls who required special care.

My older sisters Yvonne, Frieda, Mona, and Dianna were already in Mission residential school, St. Mary's, when my brothers began their families in Kilgard. My sisters' lovely children came later. So many children kept coming! June, my elder sister-cousin, was married in the U.S. The oldest, Rena, who was my first cousin but raised like a big sister in our family, was married and away in Chilliwack birthing twelve children, some before I was born. I liked everyone having many children but of course I didn't realize the hard times that came with many children. Especially in getting about with so many. Cars were not as prevalent as they are today. We did not just up and drive off so easily. I rarely saw my older siblings but I knew who was who and I loved them all: I was so happy when they came home. It was good! I remember happily running to my oldest brother Ray's house when I would see their cars there; very few of our people had vehicles then.

One time I went running into the house happy to see June and her family at Ray's. My brother Dave, who didn't have children yet, looked at me hard, so I stopped in my tracks questioningly. He said, "Eeehe, Where's your hanky TSheh'?" I looked down at my shoulder where mom always pinned a clean little piece of one of my baby brother Ike's old cloth diapers; it was my nose-diaper she joked. "Oh, no!" I thought quickly. "It is gone! Now I'm in for it." It must have fallen off in my haste to see my big sister June and whatever surprises awaited! Thinking fast because, like my dad, my brothers watched over us younger kids, I quickly reached down and picked up the hem of my dress instead, eager to please and not to be grossly snotty in front of my adult family. I blew my nose into it – hard! They watched in surprise, chuckling at my desperate attempt to make my nose clean. I was relieved when they burst out laughing and June gave me her hanky, saying, "Don't be so mean to her." I was cautious about keeping my little hanky pinned to my shoulder after that.

I felt cared-for by my huge family, this was my home.

Our family situations back then bore no intergenerational effects of residential school that I was aware of at the time. Not until later. My older sisters were always in residential school so they missed these visits I had with older siblings and relatives. It made me eagerly look forward to joining the big sisters in that school they never ever talked about at home. Whatever they were doing there must be even more important than these family visits and business!

Chapter Three

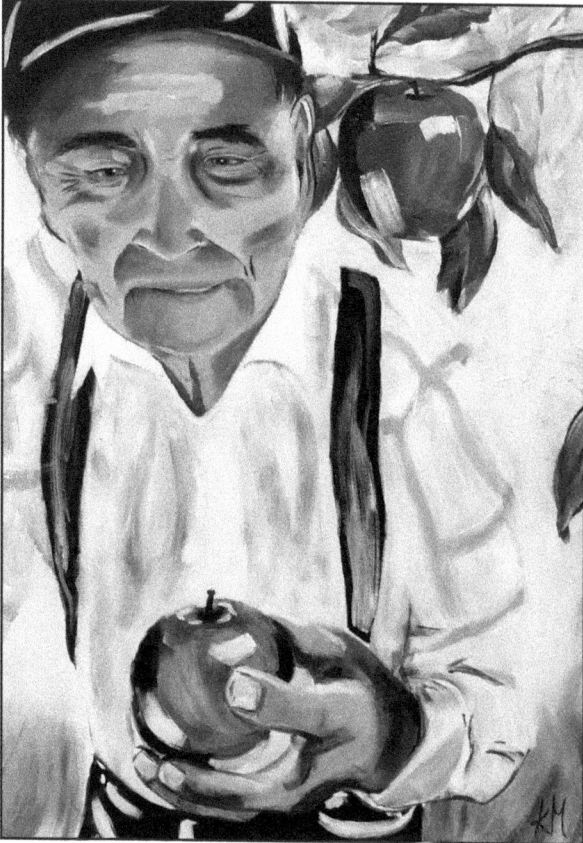

Life As I Knew It Was Changing

"Ray"

Alas, I didn't realize that soon my life would change drastically. I would follow my siblings' footsteps, be taken from my home and put into residential school, at seven years of age. Mom said I was older when I went to school than my older brothers and sisters had been when they first went to school; it seems the authorities didn't realize there were more kids at our home for them to pick up. I wanted to be with my big sisters but little did I know about where they were or what it all entailed.

My family members had all been placed in residential schools and they carried the results of traumatic experiences that were not always visible. At least that trauma was not visible to me, not then. I see now that so many feelings and experiences were desperately hidden. Our family relationships were nothing like the foreign school text books "Dick and Jane" – early school readers which teachers tried to teach me to read from. Strange baby stories made up our reading program. These I learned to read in a snap, and found horribly boring even in grade one.

Strangely, my grade one teacher did not recognize that reading came easily to me. She was a First Nations woman from a nearby reserve, but that was not to be discussed. Her teaching style bore no warmth and her methods were strictly authoritarian, as prescribed by an unfamiliar pedagogy. The classroom teacher's personal touch was absent, like most supervisors there. Encouragement of experiential or holistic learning, or enquiry methods that make learning enjoyable and progressive, did not exist in Indian Residential School teachers. They used punishment – including corporal punish-

23

ment – to make us learn. The curriculum taught was very foreign indeed. Strange readers such as Dick and Jane were our only reading materials, written about perfect white families.

No, I did not – nor did my siblings and reserve friends – play in pretty dress clothes and our parents didn't wear suits and tailored dresses with high heels. I didn't run about carrying a fluffy cute teddy bear named Tim, I didn't have a cat named Puff, and we did not have a perfectly behaved dog named Spot. My home life was very different, quite the opposite, of Dick and Jane's home life. We had a few pets but that was at my Aunt and Uncle's homestead in Leq'á:mel, Deroche. On our Summer breaks we went to their home and lived there happily and carefree. Away from the horrors of St. Mary's Indian Residential School.

My Aunty Annie and Uncle Alfred in Deroche – now called Leq'á:mel – lived a quiet life with a few animals I loved. They had a loveable scruffy dog called Buster who I looked forward to seeing every Summer in Leq'á:mel. My aunt and uncle's totally humble home in Leq'á:mel was home to me too. Once Leq'á:mel and Kilgard were one reserve but the government divided us.

My aunt and uncle had a huge farm setting to roam carefree within. I spent many hours with Buster our dog. I ran about so much with that dog I fell and badly broke my arm. I can still see my young-adult brother-cousin Merle coming back to the house looking very forlorn after many hours out to neighbours all around, he could not find anyone who would drive me the twenty miles or so to the hospital. So there I remained without medical attention all Summer, except for the comfort my mom and aunt could give me. Today my good doctor says it can be repaired now, but why? After many years of self consciousness and being made fun of, I'm comfortable with my physical flaws, they are part of me. I am who I am and proud to be who I am. I miss those days of long ago, being carefree, enjoying food from the backyard and fresh wholesome milk from my aunt and uncle's productive cow, Beauty. Her good milk was used in much of our foods.

We ate traditional foods especially wild vegetables foraged for in nearby woods. We now call those foods medicine. Mom and Auntie Annie worked hard together picking stinging nettles, berries, shoots and other vegetation to make delicious and healthy meals for all of us while dad and Uncle Alfred worked hard. Uncle Alfred had two horses, Prince and Princess, which he made great use of in his fields. They plowed the ground and dad and Uncle Alfred used their help in logging the trees. By the time I clearly remember them, the beautiful Clydesdale horses had been put out to pasture and served as pets for us to ride bareback or to just sit with.

All that which was joyful and comfortable and familiar to me, I was soon to realize, would become very distant: only memories to hold close. But I would hold them close, and I would need them more than anything.

Chapter Four

My Big Brothers Prepared Me For That Place

"Learning to Box"

My dad and big brothers were the authority figures and made sure they took charge of us in various ways for various reasons. Early on, my brothers taught my sisters to box and often held boxing matches with neighbourhood cousins. My sisters were tough and I tried hard to be tough too. They would win matches easily.

My brothers would get out their boxing gloves for their "fights." Brother Dave had one more boxing match before becoming professional, but left home for work and never made that match. To me he was a handsome, loving hero who was very good to me. But then all my brothers were, and each had his own way of showing it. They liked to train us kids to box and defend ourselves, when they were home. Now I think the training was because they knew what we would face in residential school, abuse from nuns and priests and sometimes from other kids. They wanted us Silvers to be tough like them.

One time my sisters told me of a particularly rowdy boxing match at our house. My older sister Mona loved boxing. She was fearless and good at it, and this one time she had a tough match with a male cousin whom she always worked hard to beat. At one knock-'em-down match she accidentally punched him right on a swollen, angry red sore on his forehead! Well unfortunately with a swift right hook it popped open, squirting blood all over the place! He hollered bloody murder! He was jumping about screaming, "my brains are falling out *owww*... My brains!!" He ran home hollering with his big old dog yowling right behind him, and the louder he howled, the louder his dog howled! So their echoing screams rose higher and higher through our quiet village! Our dad

29

gave them all big trouble over that. Needless to say everyone was okay; it was just another bit of excitement on our otherwise quiet reserve.

In Kilgard us younger kids stuck together, played, fought and protected one another. Four families made up our little Sumas First Nation, referred to then as Kilgard. Char Ned was my best buddy. I was often with her sisters, my cousin Meh, and my older nieces: my brother Ray's girls. The Kelly twins were quiet but made their mark in our group.

Char and I played often with the twins, I favoured John and she favoured Hugh. We often sat in the creek culvert and shared penny candies we bought from collecting and selling bottles. It was hard to tell the twins apart, even their family mixed them up. I would ask which one is John? Then I would make sure I sat beside him. Maybe he was favoured because he let me eat more candies or perhaps because he never talked back to me when I gave advice or voiced my thoughts anytime anywhere.

Then there was a bigger, silent neighbour who was most often in the fields helping his dad with their cows. He was too quiet to really join in our games and fun. He couldn't be bothered with our shenanigans. Sometimes when I wanted to see and play with more friends I hiked down to see the neighbour boy. I would follow him as he collected the cows for milking, using some type of big stick chasing after those cows shouting, "heeyaaa, get!" Feeling this was a pretty important job to have, I'd run behind him going "heeyaa," too. One day as I followed him I asked for a big yellow apple from his tree. Being friendly and strong he climbed way up the big crooked tree and got me a plump yellow apple. I munched happily, running behind him and examining the apple. I asked, "why are there clear juicy spots in this apple?" He simply said, impatiently, "it's just honey, it's good, eat it," and ran off to do his chores alone. The boy spoke few words and if you didn't like that, tough; move on. It was the last time I saw this friend for a long while. We didn't know each other much after I was put into the school, an event which I did not know would take place later that same year. It was a long while later, during young adulthood, before I saw him again or visited with him. I did not get to be with the entire Kelly family in Kilgard until later years.

My favourite playground in Kilgard was my parents' field where a white farmer named Charlie let his cows roam everywhere. Not because I played with the cows, but because there, all by itself near the creeek, was a huge cedar tree spreading out its thick branches. My friends and I often played on it and up it and under it. We could easily climb up because its branches hung low to the ground, shaped like enveloping brown arms. We could use it as a look-out or just lay in those arms, up off the ground, talking or playing "pretend." In June we could pick cherries and later in summer we could pick apples from our orchard, and the tree hid us well as we sat up there munching.

During one of our "war" games, during which cousin Meh was always the Sergeant, I was perched up high on a crooked branch where I thought I was safe from surprise attack. But a surprise was in store for me. The gang concluded their battle and suddenly scooted down the tree to leave. I hurried to follow, and got my dress stuck on an unfamiliar branch! I jostled and jerked it as hard as I could while trying to keep my balance. But I was stuck tight. I pulled with all my might - swinging and pulling and yelling, I grabbed a lower branch and pulled myself almost upside down. Then I pulled at my dress with the other hand and put all my weight into it. I heard *ripping* and *swishing* which I ignored. Then *Rip! Bang! Crash!* I went tumbling down to the next rough branch. I shimmied down to the lowest armchair-like branch, my once-pretty dress in tatters. It had been carefully made from flower-printed rice sacks by my mother, but now it was torn half off and hanging every which-way. I was very worried that I would be in trouble because mom worked hard to make us decent clothes in those days. I held my dress together and jaunted across the field, slipping on cow pies as I went. I guess I looked too comical for my mom to give me heck, so I got off lightly - and my dad wasn't around to see me.

That big, beautiful cedar tree still sits in the field. I'm sure it holds a hundred years of memories and I hope it stays there another hundred years. Cedar trees provide many things for Sto:lo people, not least a special kind of protection.

Chapter Five

It Was Time

"Coming Home"

One day as I was playing house with Char and making mud pies, pies we actually sampled sometimes, mom called me inside. She said, "You're going to be with your older sisters at St. Mary's school." I jumped for joy, saying: "Oh boy yay I get to be with them now!" All I knew was that they were away most of the time and I wanted to be wherever they were.

My sisters Frieda, Mona and Dianne were already there and my big sister Yvonne was finished school by then but she was away from home. I remember getting a square cloth of sorts as I saw mom do to pack some of our belongings in when we had to run to Aunty Dolly's or Aunty Edna's in a hurry. I gathered my possessions which were few and tied them neatly inside as I saw my mom do, then tied the four corners as she did. "There," I thought, "I'm ready to go to the school with my big sisters." It was a completely mysterious place at the time. Mom didn't take those few skimpy things of mine, only what I wore to that school. A simple pink cotton dress with rose buds on it.

Uncle Clarence owned a car so the priests allowed him to take his daughter Char and me to the big old white cement building way up the hill in Mission City, where we had never been before.

I was excited and could hardly contain myself, I would soon see my big sisters, or so I thought. Mom didn't tell me what I would face once I arrived. Nobody did. My sisters and brothers never talked of residential school in front of me, ever. I happily got ready for this adventure.

Several of us piled into that little old car and took off in a pile of smoke trailing behind us down the homemade rugged driveway: "Here we come, St Mary's! On our way to Mission at last!" I could hardly wait to see my big sisters who were always away, living at that mysterious place most of the time!

Once parked outside the big old building, my mom gathered me up and took me inside. I was immediately taken away from my mom and led coldly into the smelly old building by a woman in a long black robe over a long white robe, a nun, a "Sister" the kids called them. My family was told to leave immediately. I only remember the feeling of abandonment. The way I was led away from my family was so abrupt, so cold, callous, and final, that I somehow knew I would not see my mom and dad for a very long time. But I thought I would see my older sisters.

Quickly I was rushed through cold dark rooms, one after another, losing sight of my cousin Charlene. The nun pushed me into a cold, dank, cement room that was smelly and stinky and unlike anything I had ever experienced before. It had many shower spouts on the walls, and there were other kids there too: ducking, crouching and crying under cold, harsh spraying water.

I was told to strip everything off and the clothes were thrown in garbage bags with all the other children's clothing, taken away to be incinerated. The nun barked at me as I tried to retrieve my little pink dress that mom lovingly sewed pink rose shaped buttons onto. They said our clothes were full of lice and vermin and "God knows what else!" I wondered how that could be, as my mother kept my few clothes hand-washed, mended and tidy.

The nun and a reluctant big girl poured thick white gloops of malodorous disinfectant all over me from head to toe. My long wavy hair was soaked in it as it ran all the way down to my legs, thighs, and even between my legs. The stinging, smelly poison ran down my body and into every crevice, all of me.

I was shocked, overwhelmed by painful feelings of anger, and I began screaming, jumping about and crying. Quickly I went into survival mode: kicking and crouching, resisting and screaming for my mom and my big sisters. The nun didn't respond except to jerk me around and continue to pour the caustic detergent over me. Then she shoved me under the shower with other frightened little girls.

Later I was given a dark, shapeless tunic and a navy blue smock to put on. Gone was my little pink cotton dress that mom had stitched a tiny plastic rose onto because I loved pretty things. I still love the colour pink and tiny pink baby roses.

I did not see my sisters at all that day or night. It turned out I rarely got to see them as we were separated according to age and grade. Everyone was given numbers and that's how they identified us; numbers some friends remember today. I do not. To me I was Beatrice Elaine Silver from Kilgard and no number could change that. I cannot and never will remember that number.

After that I remember the cold, smelly, cement dining room which was so foreign to me. At home we ate together and if we had more people than could fit around the dining table, mom placed us kids on the long stairway which was fun. We had stairs leading to the attic rooms and the wood stairs served as our table and seat; we could see our family around our big old round oak table. The chairs were oak with swirling wrought iron backs, and dad's was bigger with horse hair stuffing: comfortable and homey. It all represented happiness and security for me.

By comparison, residential school meal times in that old school were unhappy, cold, tasteless times to say the least. The food was the worst mess of unappetizing food I had ever seen. I soon learned that if we didn't eat the slop served to us we were punished and starved. I endured both beatings and starvation. The food we didn't eat was continually dumped into the next meal: porridge, milk, bread, anything left over. It eventually became sour and bubbly and I doubt that even starving animals would eat it.

The very stern superior supervisor sat in front of our tables with his huge tray laden with delicious looking food. Mr. Gerald Moran hit us constantly, especially me, if we even looked at him. Whether we looked at him with a smile or in fear, we were hit. I glared back and spoke nasty words at him because I could take his hits. It was worth it to me. He took pleasure in leaving his high positioned comfortable seat to march over to hit me or one of us even if we were only laughing, although laughing and fun was rare, mind you. He never smiled, himself.

The junior boys and girls ate in the same room on separate sides of the cement hall, not allowed to speak to each other. I remember a favourite classmate of mine, Cameron, who tried to take a small amount of peanut butter out of the cafeteria in a little piece of paper of sorts for nourishment later. We were always hungry. Some little kids cried of hunger at night, as Cameron did. Mr. Moran took him to the middle of that big room and strapped him until his little hands bled and his little face scrunched in pain. There was nothing he or we could do and nowhere to run in that cold, foul smelling little cement room. I watched with helpless sadness as Cameron crouched and cried. I so wished that I was grown up so I could hit the supervisor with a chair or worse. Mr. Moran, to me, was truly evil.

Another time a little girl who was severely disabled was sick during our Sunday wiener-and-bean dinner and threw up into her food. Mr. Moran got angry with her, ignoring her illness, and attempted to force her to eat it. Her vomit was mixed in with beans, of course she got sicker and was punished for that by being sent out to the dungeon. I still cry about what Cameron, Carol and I, and many more innocent children experienced. I can only cry and try to forgive and move on.

I tried to locate Cameron and Carol, but I received mixed information. I hope they are enjoying what makes them happy now.

As for the dreaded Mr. Moran, I saw him on a Vancouver news channel years ago, in my early teaching years, shaking his fist at a cameramen. He was charged, tried and sentenced for several sexual abuses he committed while I was in that school. He gave boys alcohol and then raped them, it was reported. I felt horrible because I was in that school then and knew the boys he abused badly.

At that time he also took pleasure in beating us, especially me who balked at his ridiculous singing lessons; one in particular where he tried to teach us to sing "I'm so pretty, witty and gaaayy!" I giggled and made fun as I couldn't contain myself at the comical musician he portrayed himself to be; his singing was growly and croaky. Mr. Moran would wring my ear right around and sharply slap my head. Eventually my ear began to bleed easily after many hits and became swollen often. Yes Moran delighted in causing me pain even if I sang as he demanded.

To this day I suffer ear aches and infections. Along with ear problems and vertigo I endure migraine headaches often. I can only imagine what Moran went through in prison, only our Creator and his spirit knows. Gerald Moran died in prison.

As far as I know, the men who charged him are all still alive and doing better with families now. In spite of the terrible abuses that were inflicted, some students I went to the old St. Mary's school remain survivors and remain friends. However, so many are not here anymore. They all have their stories, it is sad that many went to the better side carrying old grievances with them. I find comfort in knowing that deceased students whom Moran intentionally hurt are in a better place, especially Cameron, Bradley and Kate.

As I write I think of my kind friend Cameron. I like to think that he is at peace with a comfortable life; he was a caring and kind boy. I also remember fondly, the first time I had to line up for shots in the old cafeteria he was beside me as I cried and firmly resisted getting that needle in my arm, as I did at home in Kilgard. I ran in circles, pulling away from the nurse. Some of the boys giggled and pointed at me which made my behaviour worse. Cameron looked at me sympathetically, telling the boys to shut up and trying to comfort me; I settled down and allowed them to give me the vaccination needle. He was a wonderful boy and I will always remember him.

That was a bit of progress for me, Cameron helping me get through that. At home when the nurse from Indian Affairs came around I fought the old army-uniformed woman alone! That was the time when old Miss Ross came puffing up our home-made trail, bumping along with her jiggling, chubby red cheeks; struggling with her worn out doctor bag; her boat-shaped hat askew and lopsided; sighing and making out-of-breath noises. After that challenge of climbing our rugged uphill trail to our home and dragging herself into our little living room, she asked my father with exasperation, "where are the children?"

My dad was visibly uncomfortable and did not know how to sooth me when he couldn't control his own nervousness about this authoritative nurse. He tried to hold me on his knee so she could innoculate me. But no, I would not have it! I pushed away and made a wide zig zag circle around them so neither the nurse nor my dad could grab me. I grabbed my tiny brother Ike and ran him out the door with me, down the steps and under the dirt crawl space before my dad could call, "Stop! Get over here!" I held my brother close and would not budge from our dark hiding spot.

We hid under the crawl space watching wide eyed as old Miss Ross in her Red Cross suit and hat tried to crouch down to summon us out. My dad was beside her and very embarrassed, not knowing what to say. So I said loudly, "Nooo! Go to hell!" Remember, I had lots of older brothers who I listened to, more than they knew. All we could see was her large bosom, tightly covered with her gray suit coat, hanging men-

acingly over us at the edge of the porch; her gloved hand trying to summon us out. Well, we stayed under there as long
as we could, knowing if our father was still close by we
would get a whipping. Now if nurse Ross and my dad were
like my friend Cameron I would have cooperated. Maybe.

At those times, I needed my mom or my older sisters
with me. My mom was in the hospital at that time and my
sisters were in the residential school. If they could not be
there with me at times like that, then I wanted to be at the
school with them.

Alas, I didn't have my older sisters to turn to for comfort and
protection when I did go to school. They happily left the old
school soon after I arrived. I remember my big sisters Frieda
and Mona being there, but I rarely saw them.

Frieda was liked by the nuns and authorities – probably
because she had long blond pretty hair. They made her the
May Queen, Sports Queen, Senior President and all that pop-
ular stuff. She says it was not as harsh for her as it was for
us, she does not say much about it. Frieda was kind to me always. Her girlfriends in Senior class were all pretty and kind
too, I liked the senior girls' attention but saw them rarely.
Most are still here and I communicate with some of my sister
Frieda's friends, like Norma Anderson Nahanie – I talk to her
and enjoy her friendship today. Donna, Judy, and others are
still active in their communities, I'm told.

My middle sister, Mona, was a tough rebel who ran away
often and got punished. What I remember being told when I
didn't see her there one day, is that she ran away. She would
always run away from that old school. They would take her
back only for her to take off again. Finally my oldest sister

and her husband were the ones to take Mona back. However, Mona had such a rebellious temper that when the nun tried to drag her into the school she wound up and kicked her full force right between the legs, causing that agitated nun to stagger around grabbing her crotch in pain and shock. Well, our big sister decided that no way could she leave her with the nun's wrath so took her right back home, ignoring the Sister Superior's objections. That certain nun was not strong physically or mentally so did not stand up to my adult sister. I was very sad when Mona went home. I didn't see her often, but the fact I knew she was close by in the school was comforting.

I remember seeing Mona, Dianna, and another Kilgard child perform for us little kids once. I was proud of my sisters' singing and dancing although I didn't know what it was about. They performed the skit that nuns had them perform for Catholic church friends from town. (By the way, when I asked her about re-telling this incident Mona said: "tell it like it like I told you!" – so I am.) The nuns laid the three girls on the floor, with their little faces painted black, then taught them to sing a horrible racist song. The girls sang, "Three little niggers layin' in bed... two were sick and the other 'most dead; they took 'em to the doctor and the doctor said: feed them niggers shortening bread." Mona told me their audience laughed and clapped watching these little Native children sing with black painted faces. They were singing lyrics they did not understand. They unhappily did what they were made to do. I get angry remembering some of that. How the nuns forced their blatant racism on innocent children is unconscionable to say the least.

In spite of a rocky road, my sister Mona turned out fine.

She has many grandchildren and still teaches our language Halkomelem to preschool children. I missed my big sister. Even if we were not allowed to visit, I knew she was there. Especially at night I needed and missed my family.

I was always lonely and afraid and I needed comfort at times, but I didn't get it. When I had a bad day or night, there was no one there. I had nightmares when disturbing things happened at the school, and they often did. For instance, our sweet kitten got squashed in our so-called "recreation room" which was cold hard cement. She was ours we felt, our own little pet. The kitten wandered into our rec room so we hid her and loved her. However, one day a class mate accidently stepped on her while jumping off a bench. I watched in horror as the kitten kicked about struggling to live. I cried many nights about that horrible tragedy. I wanted my sisters but I was not allowed to see them.

That night I had nightmares all night and kept the supervisor awake. She informed Sister Agatha, who happened to be her older biological sister. The next morning Sister Agatha took me outside and bawled me out and threatened to strap me if I ever bothered her little sister, also named Agatha, ever again. Her little sister was exhausted because of my silly nightmares, so that old mean nun said that I should be ashamed of myself for being a sissy. At that school, comfort for children was not a requirement or a desire for supervisors to provide.

That sad experience gave rise to traits within me that I value to this day. I cannot tolerate child abuse nor animal abuse. I react whole-heartedly to all kinds of abuse: violence of any kind gives me a sick, terrifying feeling that makes me feel helpless. But not for long. I quickly learned to defend others in need, be they people or animals. I was always ready to assist others but I reacted differently when I was abused, as if I believed I did something to deserve the abuse. I used to respond with a glaring still silence at abusers who came toward me. Now I find I react to abuses toward myself more appropriately. I was only ever the protector of others in various situations if needed. Now I feel I am important too. We are gifts here and our earth and all within it are gifts. I have learned that the Creator's creations deserve love, respect, care and honour. In their own ways my siblings and parents gave that to me and I hope I always give it in return.

My sister Dianna stayed a bit longer in the school with me and went on to the new school that the church and government built on top of the hill. Alas, she was not with me long at that new school. She left as soon as she could, like most kids did.

Dianna was barely four years old when they took her to the residential school. She tells of the sadness she experienced, being so young in that school and very much alone. My sister Dianna says she roamed the big school grounds alone daily, not allowed in the classrooms. She said she would peek into the classroom windows that she could barely reach: she would stand on tip-toe enough to peer in. Nobody of authority took the time to look after her or check on her all day, or see to her health and safety. The buildings were far apart and no one saw where she wandered into alone. She told us of the horrors she often witnessed in those buildings, sights that no child – or anyone, for that matter – should witness.

Dianna asked me not to share those experiences here so I respect her wishes. I don't know what her young innocent mind thought as she roamed about seeing scary things in and out of the old school buildings; the carried horror stories that haunt us still. Hearing her story today, I can only say it makes me cry. The feelings and confusion that arose as she looked in with tender eyes can only be imagined. Seeing the deserted unclean grave yard right next to our playground which carried many sorrowful stories and haunting secrets, I can only imagine. Years later I looked there at the old uncared for cemetery too as with classmates I stayed close to. It was filled with tiny old iron crosses that we knew were the only markings of the little children who died tragically there. And those were many.

Children also died in the old school while I was there. We began to recognize the signs when there had been a death. Before the morning prayer classes, teachers would tell the departed student's classmates that they had had to go home during the night.

In the old school, my little brother Ike said he saw the priests carrying a school mate, Bradley Smith, from the dormitory late one night, and he never showed up in class ever again. Bradley was a big boy to me at the time but he was only a little boy in grade four; a friendly, boisterous boy. His sister Kate was not informed properly or taken care of when her brother died. Like my family and many others, her feelings were not respected in any way.

These Disappearances of classmates were common and carried on into the new school we later moved to. Beside that historical scary graveyard was our playground, silent of what the cemetery represented. We did not completely absorb the meaning of the graves there – marked and unmarked. Rather I, along with the other children, focused on what games we could find enjoyment playing in the playground.

We would get big old cardboard boxes and slide down the grassy long slope. Over and over we slid, laughing and seeing who could reach the bottom first. We used the boxes consigned to the incinerator bins, that once held school uniforms, shoes and the like, brought in for students and supervisors. We fixed them like sleds and they suited our needs for joy riding. Sometimes we ran over bushes and tumbled by garter snakes but we didn't care. It felt good to fly down that hill because it gave me a feeling of freedom, away from it all. It reminded me of home when my older siblings and cousins flew down the old Kilgard road on the neighbour farmer's dilapidated hay wagon when he wasn't around. In spite of the horrors that school brought to me, there were some fun times with each other which I remember fondly today.

Once the school brought in a part of the Girl Guides program. It was awesome having something different! I think fondly of the Brownies Program that was uplifting and fun! Someone brought it to our school when I was in grade three. We were so happy and proud to join this group, how exciting for us! Maureen Mo Saul, Ruth Rhoda Peters, Mable Mopsey, Ruth T. and more, found the Brownies program exhilarating as we had so little to look forward to. We went off to our first meeting in an old classroom where we met Miss Tawnie Owl and Miss Brownie Owl, wow! We were happy and surprised to find that they were very kind to us. We were 'Tweenies first, learning their rules and regulations and songs. Later we received lovely uniforms with unique neck ties which we learned to tie and fold and wear properly. We graduated to become full-fledged Brownies with Elf Badges of honour. We were happy going off for hikes and a big outing with Brownies from town who all watched us curiously, but I didn't care! I enjoyed the wiener roast, the pledges and the feeling of belonging to an important group. I participated whole heartedly. Miss Tawnie Owl introduced us to the meaning of entrepreneurship and what business meant. We joyfully sold cookies in fulfilment of our lessons.

I was taken to town in my Brownie uniform and carrying loads of boxed cookies. I happily knocked on doors asking, "how many boxes would you like today?" with a big smile. They bought and bought! The girls' supervisor pulled up in town pointing to a business door for me to go into and she said do not forget to ask, "How many boxes would you like, Sir or Ma'am?" Well, I happily went skipping in to the shop where a big guy stood behind the counter. Behind him were rows of bottles of all kinds, colours and shapes. I asked him, in a very business-like manner, "How many boxes of cookies would you like, Sir?" His smile was big and kind, chuckling and clucking, and he bought two boxes. The supervisor was frantic but laughing hard: "You aren't allowed in there! That's the liquor store, Beatrice! I meant the next shop, I meant the dry cleaners!"

I sold the most cookies and got an ice cream but, you know what? I never once got one of those cookies! I don't care for cookies today unless they're Girl Guide cookies. That was a wonderful few months in the old school! However... Alas of all Alases... our beloved Brownie program was discontinued shortly after. Miss Brownie Owl reported that her program was finished and there was no leader to carry on with Girl Guides. My Brownie mates and I had each other and remained good friends. We had found new games to play together when we weren't doing chores.

Chapter Six

Religion Ruled In St. Mary's School

"First Communion"

They called themselves "God's workers," the priests, brothers, nuns and lay people who worked for the Catholic Church and the Indian Affairs Department that controlled all our people and reservations. Attending church consistently was mandatory. Indeed, it was not only their religion but their law. At least they made it *our* law.

Sunday Mass was a sacred ritual and a requirement we abided by, come hell or high water. We attended Mass, along with any other Catholic services deemed important. I dreaded those ceremonies that held no meaning for me except the chance to watch others' behaviours in the church. From observing whole-hearted praying, to the big girls and boys looking at and performing for each other, it was entertaining indeed. Loudly chanting words I didn't understand over and over made no sense to me and made me sleepy after a bit.

Heaven forbid if I fell asleep on the church bench! My ears would be savagely pulled out of shape, I learned quickly. Sitting, kneeling, standing repeatedly, hundreds of times in two hours, I used to wonder if God got tired of hearing the monotonous chants and words day after day, over and over... I often made up my own words as prayers went on: "holey Mary mother of God... hollow is thy name... fruit of thy room for Jesus..." Who really knew what they meant anyway? Did he listen? Did it bring me closer to him? Whoever he was, I feared him.

The daily catechism classes we had to listen to and the constant preaching of "God's workers" always put the fear of God in us. The religious ones said forcefully that God would punish us as fast as lightning if we were naughty or thought bad things. So when I deemed it necessary, I would quickly try to apologize to God and change my unsavory words, behaviour, or thoughts, hoping that it sufficed. After all, God forgave all sins didn't he? In my mind, talking of important things to friends and adults who cared and who I could actually see was more reasonable to me. By the end of mass my knees had red circles on them and my face held scrunchy frowns which I still try to erase today.

One day I endeavoured to test the lightning. My friends and I were sliding down the steep hill beside the graveyard – one of our usual Sunday playground activities – when Mabel slid over a tangled mass of snakes! We stopped to inspect them, and discussed what the nuns always said: the devil comes in the form of a snake. I loathe snakes, but I said to my friends, "Let's take these snakes into church and see what God does to them." So I got Mabel and another girl to fill their pockets with the snakes, right before evening benediction. That's when Father swirls his golden pot around to spread smoke, blessing and cleansing us all.

So in we went, the other girls carrying the hidden, wiggling snakes because I wouldn't touch them, much less carry them. The Holy Benediction began, very solemn, when a few snakes wiggled out of Mabel's pocket! Everyone screamed abut, jumping and creating a disturbing – but hilarious – commotion in the quiet church. We caught the snakes and got them back into Mabel's pockets, we were marched out of church and punished as usual, but nothing happened to the snakes!

All the grade one children had consistent and strict preparations for our First Communion in the Catholic Church which initiated us into true Catholicism. We would receive the holy host, which represented God, and be truly one of his children. We prayed profusely to wash our sins away day and night before bed. Venial sins and mortal sins were preached about over and over. Venial sins were little, like telling little lies; mortal sins were big, like murder or blasphemy. Holy! I was afraid to do anything, for fear of God's wrath. We chanted the rosary daily and listened to the nuns read the bible to us. The priest came in to prepare us for confession time, which was very crucial to becoming true Catholics. He and the nuns hammered away passionately and annoyingly the beauty of God, the wrath of God, the evilness and craftiness of the devil. Lord! I became leery of everything I did!

Our first official confessions happened on a Saturday, one day before Communion. I prayed and was careful not to commit any more sins after confession, at least not until after Holy Communion. The nuns and priests were adamant that we be thoroughly cleansed before receiving the holiest piece of bread which represented God. The big Communion day on Sunday was utterly and divinely important they said. I wondered why and how we could swallow God who was in that little host. I guessed I had better prepare, because who knew what could happen once I ate God. Well... I had to think real hard about all my sins: acting out, bad behaviour, swearing, fighting, and of course bad thoughts to tell Father in the little dark confessional. I had to be accepted by God or face the fires of hell. I decided I would be as pure as possible to receive Holy Communion. That little white flat piece of bread the nuns called the host was really God, whom we were about to eat because then he would be inside us! I wondered what he would taste like. We had to have Holy Communion to be purified of our sins totally and become true Catholics.

I spent many hours preparing in my mind for this big day. I thought long and hard about my sins, carefully categorizing them in order from venial sins to mortal sins, and considered what might not be worth confessing to the priest. However, just in case, I ended up adding some sins in case the priest should need to hear more. Hmmmm… by doing so did I just add another sin? It didn't matter. It was important that I receive total absolution, forgiveness, to receive that valuable host.

The Communion day was special in a more tangible way when we were given a little white Bible to carry, and a holy picture. After a rather nice – and unusual – breakfast, the little Bible was taken away again. I happily talked with the other little girls dressed in fluffy white dresses and veils bought by parents who could afford the luxury. My parents could not afford the luxury of fancy dresses. It made me sad but I was happy with the little dress I finally did get.

One pretty little dainty girl was dressed very lovely with white organza, flouncy lacy veil, lace gloves, and ruffles galore: like a little bride. She was from Port Douglas where her dad worked steadily so she always had the loveliest of everything. She was tiny and sweet with big doe-eyes that always smiled at everyone. I watched her longingly as she danced happily about getting ready to walk down the Communion aisle. I chatted around outside the chapel in my little white plain dress with tiny tulips on it and a faded limp veil which I was sure had been worn a hundred times by little girls like me. But you know what?! I felt pretty and special no matter what, proudly wearing the dress my big sister Rena Silver

Point lovingly made for me. The material was pretty and probably came from bits of wedding dress material she had. Rena could make an old hopsack look pretty with her creative sewing skills.

I was so happy that my special handmade Communion dress was delivered just in time by my big brother Herman, who came barreling up to the old school in one of his loud jalopies banging and snorting black smoke. One of the girls excitedly called me and I went out to the big yard happy to see him. "Here," he said gruffly. "Rena sent me to give you this." He tossed it out to me, not even in a bag, with a few quarters and rumbled off in his loud car leaving a trail of smoke. He seemed eager to leave the school and, more than likely his old memories as well, in the dust. My sister had to wash the dress as it had oil spots on it from his old car. No matter, I was happy to see him and the pretty dress I had been sure I would not have in time, plus getting fifty cents was pretty good too. That first Communion ceremony was a highlight of my early years at that dank old school.

I think now it was meaningful because I was treated special for a short time, but mainly it was because I felt I earned something through my own hard work. Yes: even if it was earning the right to be Catholic, which is a religion – and a religion I have long since abandoned. It was the evolvement of my actions and determination to succeed at whatever I chose to undertake that awoke me and gave me pride. Earning the right to own something and to achieve encouraged me to form a solid foundation which guides me to this day. It is a part of myself. I was discovering goals, action, evaluation, truth, loyalty, conviction, commitment and determination, and that drives me in all that I do.

Today my belief is that I can pray anywhere anytime and it does not have to be chanting words or prayers from the Bible. I talk to the Creator, I call on my good ancestors often, and I live a good life. I value honesty, kindness, compassion, and love. That to me is a "good" religion, leading a good life. Therefore, that long preparation and ceremonial process was beneficial for me. It helped to shape and chisel away at my character, making me who I am today.

I believe that people who cherish and practice their religious beliefs healthily are within their rights to do so. Good for them. If religion makes their lives happier, more peaceful and more in tune with their good environment, then that is a positive thing. A niece who I love is a Catholic with strong religious practices. She prays daily for us all, especially when there are difficulties or tragedies in our family and community. She often tells me she prays hard for our leadership so our community will progress. I respect and appreciate that. Often our people turn to her for prayers and strength when problems arise.

I chuckle now, thinking of another family member who told me once: "When things get so damn tough on the reserve, I pray to beat hell!" However, many residential school survivors have not forgiven religious orders for controlling us and serving as the cold upper hand for the Canadian government. Their ultimate goal was to destroy "The Indian's way of life," so they could better manage us; control us and everything we stood for. Too well we realize the effects of colonization today.

Chapter Seven

The Wall Was A Bridge

"Where Is My Brother?"

An important goal the residential school pursued, and enforced with an iron fist, was the act of dividing siblings, cousins, and friends. Girls had their "side" and the boys had theirs. One did not cross over the line without dire consequences. In spite of those immediately sufferable punishments, we often did what we had to in order just to see our relatives and friends. Given the circumstances, I think we were constantly anxious for proof of wellbeing, or at least life. We looked for each other in playgrounds and dining rooms which, although separate, we could see one another in across the way. We had minimal human contact except with stern, stoic teachers in classrooms empty of learning material, where interaction was minimal. The exception was in the gymnasium during basketball and other games. During basketball games supervision was loose as the supervisors were coaching, or as supervisors took those times as free time and disappeared. I liked those times because I could see male cousins and others not in my division, the junior girl section.

One rare time I met my cousin Meh` Melvin Williams from my reserve. During the Seniors' basketball game in the gym where everyone got to scatter during intermission, I went over to talk to him and he joked with me about my shiny black leather shoes. They had straps and little bows and were big on me. He took his shoes off and I gave him my big shoes to try on. Meh' skipped all around the gym in them, occasionally genuflecting as he skipped. I laughed so hard as he skipped, keeping a serious face but also wearing a funny smile, drawing laughter from the girls and boys. I was so happy when I got to see Melvin and other cousin friends in the school.

Seeing one another was painfully rare and random. At times we could see the boys directly across from our rec room window that faced theirs. We would watch, make faces and signs, and wave at each other. I would often go to that big window when I was lonely and longing for home: just a glimpse of my cousin Melvin or a familiar friend or family member was somewhat comforting against the loneliness and separation.

Although the boys' and girls' playgrounds were separated by huge fields and buildings, we managed to sneak close enough to visit each other briefly or at least wave and shout when authorities were not visible. The boys played marbles and I found the game appealing. I occasionally managed to get close enough to watch and sneak a marble roll or two. Some boys would allow us girls to play while others would not have it. Well, I did what I wanted usually so I had no other choice but to budge my way in, take a cobb, and shoot the pretty marbles. I ended up with a marble collection which I shared with the girls. Those marbles were valuable as we didn't have toys. The boys tolerated me and didn't fight to keep me out of their games. Perhaps that was easier than tangling with me!

Sometimes I would just walk along the edge of the dividing field to look out for my little brother or cousins. At times I went with girlfriends and sometimes I went alone.

Once in a while I would be lucky enough to see them. I used to watch particularly for my very quiet, sad, cousin-nephew Murray because he was always alone. I didn't want him to be alone so much and I felt his aloneness keenly. He would walk along wearing his warm Elmer Fudd hat with the ear flaps swaying as he idly kicked stones about. I would try to get his attention by hollering and waving, but if he saw me he didn't let on, he silently walked on. I wondered what Murray was thinking and so wished I could talk to him. He was often alone there and I remember him looking forlorn most times. I was unhappy too but always reached out to classmates and organized games of some sort. I'm not sure why, but I always had something to bring my friends out of that situation and remind them of who we really are and what's good in life.

Many of my fellow students turned inward. Murray in particular. Because we were closely related I thought he would respond to me. But no, he remained silent there at St. Mary's school. My cousin-sister June used to bring her children to her home in Kilgard so we got to know them. Both Murray and Joyce, her oldest children, attended the school with me. Both went on to be responsible hard working adults in the United States. Sadly both have gone to the better side, joining their parents there.

I treasure the memories with my family. Murray's mom was my older cousin June Silver Boome who was raised as my big sister; she was indeed my big sister. June paid special attention to us. Once she took my older sister Frieda to the U.S. for the summer before I attended school. My sister Mona said she brought her home all decked out nicely with new clothes and shoes. My sister Mona said, "Gee you got new everything! ...and I don't even have bloomers to wear!" Mom made our underwear and dresses so I'm sure she meant new underwear. June and mom got a charge over that remark. My sisters were not shy in the least, therefore they said what was on their minds most often. Frieda was more silent and very lady-like, opposite from the rest of us. We don't know what she is feeling unless she is perturbed and riled up over something, which is rare. My sister Frieda is still quiet today.

Unfortunately many surviving students remain silent today, they do not expose their true feelings, while others of us tell our stories, knowing it helps with the long healing process of going on with life. As I spoke to fellow classmates while writing my story, I found that most have shared their stories and feelings, and they gave permission for me to print their names. Others were not ready to discuss residential school experiences or to have their experiences recalled by others. A few could not remember and were nervous to talk about experiences. A few more survivors still cry sadly and cannot discuss residential school. A few got angry saying that what we went through there, all that garbage, is nobody's business. And to leave it alone. Troubled memories brought out too much hurt and anger. They prefer to leave it back there, way back there.

I can see by talking to many fellow students about St. Mary's school, and by talking to older school survivors, I have opened the door slightly. Hopefully more schoolmates begin sharing and releasing old pain from residential school.

They reminded me of our classrooms being restricted places but the girls and boys shared classrooms. Primary school was strange at first – it was so unlike my home. The grade one teacher was cold and didn't provide a good experience for me. She was rigid and too snippy toward me. She was expecting little from me, so I gave her little. I don't remember much of that first year in class except that teacher failed me, which gave me another year with her. Most of those teachers failed me because of my rebellion. However, early on when I was ready, I began reading: reading everything in sight! Boring senseless old Dick and Jane books I whipped through in a brief sitting regardless of page by page reading lessons. They were such foreign stories to me however; at home we didn't have perfect families. Dick and Jane's mother was in starched dresses usually blue and white, father in suit and tie with a brief case always. Sally and Dick were always perfectly behaved and tidy. Even Puff the orange cat, Spot the dog and Tim the teddy were perfect family members indeed. No matter, I flew through those baby books.

By grade two a rather caring teacher, Sister Michael, often had me read aloud to the class. When she went out of class for long periods she gave me books to read to the kids, and when those ran out I took the Bible she left me with and read that aloud too. Mind you, I didn't have a clue what I was reading nor did the kids who looked at me quizzically with their bright eyes, but I carried on reading aloud and reading as much and as often as possible – hoping the teacher would stay away longer. We never knew where our teacher went for those breaks of hers. Today, knowing what I know now, I can only imagine and giggle, or be horrified, depending on stories I've been told. Many teachers did the same there, taking mystery breaks.

The awesome thing in those early years was that I learned to read and love it. I look back and remember Sister Michael, who was kind to me and most of all she believed in my skills. I got scolded often, yes, but those scoldings contained words like, "I know you can do better Beatrice! ...you are so smart ...that's going to waste! ..." That kind little nun's true words hit the right place, those words stuck with me to this day. Just as my mother's constant story telling did. My mom said she always knew I was a tough survivor and realized early that I would do okay in the world.

I know and realize now what I didn't know then. Jean, my kind, quiet, humble mother, knew all along deep down that I would have a bumpy journey but would come out just fine.

At our home my mom told me stories all the time. I would beg her to tell me the Wild Woman From The Mountain story, Toq'we'ia. She was patient and I'm sure got tired of telling that story but she told it over and over again. I loved the story and the comfort her voice brought to me.

Mom was illiterate. Teachers in Kuper Island Residential School did not teach her to read. She had a story telling gift which was magnificent for me. My dad always read. I am not sure what, but I would see him reading. Once in a while when he was in the mood for it, I would lay beside him hoping he would read to me. Occasionally he would show me comic pictures and add silly words to the captions and make me laugh. But it was mom's story telling that inspired me to learn printed words, what they meant, and to write them on paper. She lovingly spent the time to give me that. I can still hear her telling me stories when I cannot sleep.

Often my mother would create stories from pictures only, or from comics the big boys left laying around. She creatively made up the stories from those pictures. These made-up stories, and seeing the joy my dad and older siblings got from reading books and comics, reinforced my desire and determination to learn to read and to write. It is the memories of my mother and her story telling that I carry as the foundation of my teaching life today. I believe my mother Jean's beautiful heart and knowing soul makes her happy on the other side. It was my Mom Jean Silver who left me a legacy to be proud of myself, no matter what the situation may be. My education indeed began at home, containing all kinds of experiences wrapped into one, some thorny and some painful and some as beautiful as a pink blooming rose.

Chapter Eight

Transfer To the New School: A Hopeful Change

"You Could Write"

The time came when authorities were ready to move us to the new St. Mary's residential school. Superiors were excitedly preparing us for it. I watched the new buildings being built when I could sneak across the field to see. Big red brick buildings went up that looked like Coqualeetza hospital to me. I was not one bit excited about that new school with huge lonely looking fields. It was humungous and, to me, even threatening. I was in middle grades by then and independent in my mind. I said and thought as I saw fit, much to the dismay of supervising nuns and priests. At times I wished I could just do as they demanded and shut my mouth. It might have been easier to just accept what was happening and go onward, but to me doing that would have been more painful than any punishment I received. And I was punished brutally and often. No way could I keep my mouth shut, I am who I am and I can only accept that; I can't be anyone or anything else.

The new school, although shiny and new, held very little change for us. Cosmetics do not change what is inside of any person or thing. My older sister and her husband drove me there the first time. Every time we crossed that old wooden train bridge I would cry. It didn't matter that I was almost ten years old; I let out wailing sobs. My sister comforted me by saying they would visit and maybe mom would let me move home to the St. Mary's day-school soon. I hoped for that.

I soon met new friends and happily many friends from the old school were there. School life was a bit different, but our treatment and their pedagogy, all that they taught us, remained the same. The only difference was that I was older and more defiant. I refused to pay attention to their lectures

71

and lessons and therefore I was always punished in and out of class. I joined with friends who were like- minded, and we were the intermediate school group that liked to cross over the restricted line, the school's arbitrary boundaries for acceptable behaviour. Normaline and her sister Yvonne were new to the school and we quickly became friends. Having family connections was comforting. Then there were the girls in my classes that I knew from the old school: Rhoda, Wanda, Maureen, and others. There was an older girl from the old school who watched out for me all the time, Kate, she looked after all of us younger girls especially when we got crazy ideas. Kate Smith was husky and tough on the outside but kind on the inside. She used to eat our food so we wouldn't get punished for hiding it to throw away later. Kate from Mount Currie was like our guardian and I cared a lot about her. Kate paid special attention to me and I liked and appreciated that a lot.

In the grade 4/5 class I had a teacher who was somewhat bearable, Mr. B., in spite of keeping a pint of whiskey in his desk. I know he did because we would snoop around when he sneaked out for a cigarette. Old Mr. B. reeked of booze and smoke continuously. I got away with a lot in his class. My friend Rhoda still laughs and says, "You used to like bugging that teacher Mr. B. all the time!" Yes, I wanted to liven up our lives! He used to grab me and push me out into the hallway in exasperation although he never strapped or hit me ever. If I continued to be defiant he would stroll me firmly but slowly out and say "What am I to do with you...?" With angry but controlled action, he would put books in each of my hands and make me hold out my arms. If I didn't cooperate fully then, I would be dragged back inside and made to kneel in front of the class. This didn't shame me in the least. By then I had developed an armour that cushioned the blows and harsh words. I was a bit passively aggressive, I realize now. Mr. B. did not worry me. Actually I felt sorry for him; he was half drunk most of the time, talking slowly while attempting to teach us Social Studies, the history of Canada. Native history was never a part of their curriculum. His classes were boring so I always worked to spice them up.

Once Rhoda and I, with a few other girls, hung around after class as he could be interesting at times. I began asking him about smoking. His fingers were stained yellow from cigarette smoke. I asked him if we could have a cigarette. Well, Mr. B. went on about our health, our ages and I had answers for each, directed back to his habit. Getting nowhere I said, "Father Dunlop wouldn't be pleased if he knew you had whiskey in your desk, Mr. B." Bawling us out and nattering on as he often did, he finally gave us a cigarette and a match – after much prodding from me, and us promising not to tell. Rhoda and the others came out to the end of the field to smoke it. We tried to smoke and it was gross! After some choking and coughing we put it out. We decided Mr. B. was trying to kill us with his poison.

We wandered off in search of further adventures. No, we never told anyone about that incident! There were more adventures we created to have some enjoyment at the new school. They provided so few activities for us. In June we occasionally went swimming in Hatzic for an hour. Whatever they provided for us was so controlled that we found our own ways to liven up our lives.

In the new school they began allowing family to take us home over night on a Saturday, with strict orders that we must be back by Sunday at four o'clock sharp or never be allowed overnight visits again. One weekend my cousin Char and I were able to go home overnight with her dad and my brother Aleck. We were so excited, home! Even going for just one night filled us with uncontainable excitement! It so happened that our families got into a little house party and we did not get back by four on Sunday, we returned later that night. We were punished and lectured. It was clearly not our fault but the supervisors didn't care about the reasons why.

I was given a cruel surprise when the annual orphans' day at Birch Bay came around; we again were so excited! We could go on the Ferris wheel and other rides; we got hot dogs and delicious baked beans for lunch, topped off with an ice cream cup – yum! It wasn't much but it was the idea of eating out. I didn't know what a restaurant was and this was pretty close, I felt. We all enjoyed that day every June!

When the day came, those of us who had been late getting back into school were informed by head supervisor Miss M., without any sign of regret, that we were not allowed to go to Birch Bay! That was one of the most rare, fun days of the entire year! I was kept behind! A couple of us had to remain in the school. We didn't have supervisors with us. Sandwiches were made and left in the cafeteria for our lunch. With no TV or anything to do, I took the girls on an excursion, wandering about in the woods making our way to the old school. We headed out for the orchard at the old school, no one saw us, and I don't think anybody cared.

There we climbed trees and had a yummy feed of slightly green cherries and salmon berry shoots we called *saskies*. We made our own fun day.

Now there were two pretty horses in the orchard where

there was long grass for them. I coaxed one to the fence with fresh grass. I climbed the fence and got on his back. Immediately he began trotting along with me holding his mane and my legs tightly embracing his sides. I gently pressed my legs against his big tummy and he galloped. We flew from one end of the orchard to the other. The ride was fast and smooth, we just glided over the grass and long brush. I hung onto the horse's mane, crouching low over his neck to avoid getting whipped by branches. I loved the feeling of flying along without a care. Freedom. A bit of freedom was exhilarating! I sometimes sneaked back to that abandoned orchard to visit the horse and ride him when I could, all alone in the quiet orchard. I love horses today and did eventually own one in Bella Coola for a time.

Chapter Nine

Punishment Led To Running Away:
My Brief Escapes

"The Orchard"

The home I loved and most of all the family and relatives I loved were becoming more estranged and more like strangers as time went on during my stay in that school. Although the word "love" was never used in our house or even in our community, I knew I was cared for and loved in spite of what the residential school tried to teach me. We had different values and life styles that their foreign society saw as incorrect, "heathen," as government officials recorded us and the church people called us. They didn't understand that my family's actions and attitude spoke "love" at all times – even if sometimes it was "tough love." My family's "tough love" was a thousand times better than the residential school's best attempt at being half-decent, and I was old enough to know which one I wanted.

Being punished for not getting back to the residential school put ideas in my mind. I started thinking, "if I'm going to be punished for not getting to the school right on time, and I could not get myself back, I may as well run away." And that is what I did, many times!

    I would hold secret meetings with girls I trusted. Friends who wanted out as bad as me joined me in my plans to run away. We knew we would get brought back – everybody who ran away always got brought back – and we knew we would be severely strapped, among other punishments, but by then that was a pretty minor deterrent if we could get free of that horrible school even for a little while. I confirmed plans with close trusted friends – Normaline, Wanda, Rhoda and another girl – about my decision to run away. We would wait until dark and run off before the bed- time bell. Supervisors didn't count heads so we figured we had time to make it past the Mission bridge. I secretly approached my senior friend Kate who always looked out for us. I told her our plan. Being protective as she was, Kate decided she must come to guide and look out for us. She met with us and discussed our plan and we prepared carefully. We took slices of bread and some apples, just whatever we could snitch from the dining hall. It was early Fall so was warm by day and cool at night. We prepared for that too.

When night fell, we met and Kate led us stealthily down the huge hill below the school. We were headed to the highway at the bottom of that hill. We crossed over it with Kate keeping a careful watch.

We stayed well to the side of the road, jumping in ditches when we saw car lights. Quietly we made our way into the off-road side fields, stopping only to rest. Finally, we came to a huge fence and a gate in one field. Kate helped each of us climb over. We got over the gate safely in the pitch dark. Then we noticed that Kate was not right behind us. We all began whispering loudly for Kate; we couldn't see her anywhere! Another girl and I began climbing back over that old gate to look for her, when we heard groaning and loud screeching! "Kate! Where are you?" I practically shouted, then I was quickly nudged by Rhoda to shush. All of a sudden *groan! squeak! ...timberrrrrrr...* CRASH! The old gate and fence cracked loudly and suddenly fell on us with a *thump!* with Kate on top of it! It was heavy! Well there was some loud protests and ouches from the girls but all were fine except for minor bruises and scrapes. Kate fell behind our little group because she had to pee, and she didn't tell us; she was the strong silent one. Kate always did what she needed to do without any fuss. I looked up to her as did the other girls.

Somehow we made it to the Mission bridge although I'm not sure how. We waited for the green light at the bridge where we heard loud, angry shouting. We could see the priest outside his car, several cars down from us, stopped at the red light. He was frantically waving and shouting, "get back here, you little devils, you!" We began running, hoping the light would turn green so we could dash over the bridge. We could see the excited, rotund priest under the street lamps, bouncing about and shouting, "Devils!" as he tried to summon us to his car. We ran! He began running! He was huffing and puffing – he was a big man – and desperately trying to coax us to turn back. Being tired and scraped and bruised, we looked at each other and thought we better go back and face the music. At least we escaped for a few hours.

We were lined up in his office upon our return and lectured profusely. Each one of us were taken into a room to be strapped soundly on our bottoms and our hands. My hands still have scars from those black snake-like straps! I swore out loud with every slap and got it worse. I wouldn't cry until I left the room. Kate got it the worst as they blamed her most, her being the oldest. Kate only came to protect us, I told the priest, but of course it didn't matter to him. The priest punished her profusely!

The next day it was told to the other students and the supervisor said it was a lesson for everyone! 'Listen to the supervisors or suffer the consequences,' they said. What few privileges we had were taken away. Kate was an awesome basketball player so they pulled her out of the games for a long while. They punished us by taking away our only bits of enjoyment we had in that school.

More "run away from school" events occurred following that memorable first attempt. However, I never did make it home. Once, my friends Normaline, her sister Von, and I made it to her Auntie Edna's in Mission town. Auntie Edna talked kindly to us, fed us, then drove us right back to the dreaded school. While we got punished again, it wasn't as harsh because Norma's Auntie Edna brought us right back and that impressed the priests and nuns.

We were so unhappy in that school we did whatever we could to get out of there. The dangers of it never occurred to me, I just ran. I knew of older students who got away and stayed away for good, like my sister Mona. I knew of some young adults who got away and much later came back to the school for revenge! My older brothers did that. One day they came up to the school, found the clergy men who tortured them, and roughed them up. That is not my way however, I chose to forgive and move on. Acting out of anger, blaming and hating can only hurt me. That's what I believe and I move onward.

Chapter Ten

Silence Is Not Golden

"Don't Tell"

The new school didn't bring any surprises or enjoyment for me. Friends became more important and I was longing for more in my life. I refused to do much school work except reading. I read everything I could get my hands on. Reading was my brief escape from harsh realities. The school library was tiny and consisted of cast-offs from the city library or donations. I even read magazines that senior girls finished with, teen material and so forth. They offered glimpses into the real world and how others lived; moreover, what other people had that I did not.

The magazines featured The Beatles who became the rage and senior students went crazy over them. I thought they were okay but to me them and their music was another world unattainable to me. But I liked reading of them. We didn't have music in the school except what they taught us or allowed us to listen to which was the most boring old *clippity-klop* music one could imagine. Once in a while we were fortunate to hear the Seniors' records belting out catchy songs, but that was rare. Those magazines that I could manage to obtain were gifts to me. If I got caught with them supervisors took them away never to be seen again. I'm sure they probably read through them.

I think of the day someone put music on over the loud speaker, great music; not the old fuddy-duddy stuff we had to listen to. I stopped what I was doing and listened and listened with joyful puzzlement and bopped around. "Who is that? Singing that cool stuff?!" I wondered. I went out into the hallway to peek into the administration lobby. There was a young priest, he put on an album he said was the Rolling Stones. Wow! I loved them immediately and totally. The song was "I can't get no satisfaction." How cool was that! I said to the priest "you play good songs Father." He was Father Powell and a very young modern guy. I liked him right away. He told me a bit about the music and the Rolling Stones as I stood and listened to it all with him. The young priest seemed to enjoy watching me completely absorbed by the Rolling Stones' rock 'n' roll bluesy music.

After that I asked to go see him when he was around and the women supervisors, thinking I was turning a new leaf, allowed me to. I felt he understood me and cared what was happening with me. That was uncommon in the residential school. Most supervisors were authoritative, not caring about my feelings.

Well, what do you know? His awesome music stopped shortly after that and Father Powell disappeared. He left the residential school, the only priest in authority whom I liked and trusted. Rumours floated around among older students but I never found out the truth. He was gone and so was his cool music. I think he was too modern and open with us, therefore the principal and others running the school needed him gone. Perhaps his influence over people like myself was not appreciated: Father Powell did not preach the bible or the wrath of God to us.

Other supervisors came and went. Most of them did not belong to the religious order. Many supervisors at this new school were young and modern and did not stay long. I could see why. They had to live by undesirably strict rules; nobody would like to live within that environment long term.

One brother of the Oblates Order came on as the Senior boys' supervisor. He didn't pay much attention to me or any of the young girls. But one night, to my surprise, I was called down to the intermediate girls' rec room. I arrived and there sat Brother T. *What on earth?* I sat down and he began talking to me about my behaviour. *What the heck,* I thought, *he doesn't even talk to me! What does he know?* He went on, talking to me softly.

He said I was coming into womanhood and he was concerned about my future. Should I carry on behaving as I was, I would end up in trouble and pregnant when I went out into the world. This kind of talk from a stranger made me nervous and uncomfortable. I did not even wear a bra yet or menstruate! As I fidgeted about he continued to talk intimately about my dangerous behaviour. I couldn't imagine what my dangerous behaviour really was; how could it lead to getting pregnant?

I listened to him drone on about changing my behaviour, waiting to be dismissed as it was my bedtime. I told him I didn't even like boys and that I would rather beat on them than be close friends with any of them. After his concerned warnings he told me I better go to bed. After that he was pleasant and kind to me out in the hallways and cafeteria, sometimes giving me little gifts of fruit. That incident was puzzling to me to say the least! I accepted his kindness but it was out of the ordinary among other students. Brother T. never did call me out to talk privately again. Years later I saw him when he became a priest. He was distant but polite. What was his intention that evening? To attempt to change my behaviour? I don't know. Nothing physical happened that I could remember. I left it at that.

Later that year I began having nightmares which I could not remember. I would wake up sweating and afraid. We slept in cubicles that held six beds and tiny cupboards for our uniforms. My good friend Maureen slept in a little cot beside me.

One night I told Maureen I was afraid to go to sleep because of the nightmares, which I could never remember. I told her of waking up early one morning to find my private parts swollen and protruding like balloons. I didn't know what happened; if I was sexually abused I didn't remember. She said that she had nightmares too. She said that in her nightmares something was putting great pressure on her back and she could not move. (Maureen gave me permission to write this.) We decided to sleep with our beds pushed together. We would sometimes hold hands and talk late into the night. Were we sexually abused and could not remember the incidents? I believe so. Our intricate minds have ways to protect us so that we can cope with tragedies. And tragedies involving our students in that school were many.

Young teen girls would be mysteriously gone in the mornings. There were two senior girls I liked who were good to us younger girls. One who was about sixteen began crying hysterically and could not stop. Her cries turned into a sad kind of whining noise. Some of us younger girls stayed by her bed as she cried and cried. The big tough supervisor heard her there, after an hour or so, and got angry with us. She told us harshly to leave and get to our own dorm. Very concerned, we went back to the intermediate dormitory, whispering with fear and dread of what may happen to her once we left. We never saw our friend again. I was told she had to go home in the middle of the night. But, home to Vancouver Island? In the middle of the night? We didn't believe that.

The same kind of incident happened to another senior girl, a very quiet shy girl who had suffered burns across her face and was disfigured by the same accident. I used to visit her while she worked in the priests' parlour room. She would give me potato chips and snacks they kept in bowls by their large TV.

One morning she didn't show up for breakfast. We were told she had an emergency at home and had to leave in the middle of the night. She also lived on an island far away that took ferries to get to, and ferries don't travel late at night, so how did she get home? We all knew authorities did not allow us to go home often and certainly not in the middle of the night. Years later when I was a young woman out of that school, friends told me this girl had got pregnant in that school and they performed an abortion on her, but she died that night and my friends who were in her dormitory witnessed it. I believe murders happened in the new school, they did not stop because we moved into a new building. Nuns and priests remained the same. If they got away with it in the old school they knew they could get away with abuse and murder in the new school.

Most of my friends there were cooperative and avoided getting into trouble. Marie W. was one of them. She abided by all the rules. She worked hard in school and was careful not to do anything to anger the supervisors. She loved basketball and played well. She was admired by other students and the nuns liked her. Marie was our May Queen and our basketball star. She always tried to reason with me in attempts to keep me out of trouble. Marie left school early before finishing. At fifteen she married a caring, decent man and had several well-cared-for kids. Somewhere along the way she turned away from all that and moved away from her family. Marie tragically passed away not long after moving away in that life change. It left me in shock to hear of the death of my friend who I jokingly called "Goody Two Shoes." One never knows what twists, turns and detours our lives take, especially after traumas of residential school.

There are many similar stories like this. But I was sure Marie had it beat; a good family woman with good values and intentions. Residential school played a huge role in influencing the direction – or lack of direction – our lives followed. Even if we refused to allow it to affect us with a huge impact during our years there, it was always sure to affect us in harsh ways later.

Chapter Eleven

I Refused To Return

"The Doll"

By the time I was thirteen going on fourteen I knew that my time at residential school was coming closer to the end. I was a young teen and beginning to realize what I wanted in life. I knew for sure I wanted to get out of that residential school, come hell or high water. There were two young female supervisors who tried to win me over but by then nothing could be said or done to change my behaviour or keep me in that school. I carried on managing to make the best of my situation there.

Miss C. and Miss R. attempted to provide events suitable for young teens. They cleared out the former staff living quarters for a pajama party sleep-over. They got a record player and we were allowed to listen to the Beatles songs but very few of the Rolling Stones. They were too wild, they said. We danced and played games while they made us waffles! Most of us never had waffles before and they were delicious. I enjoyed that setting with my girlfriends. Miss C. and Miss R. did try to give us a taste of what we were missing out on as early teens. I appreciated that very much! It helped ease my deep longing to go home, but only temporarily. That longing to leave Mission was always inside, even though life at home had long since changed: mom had moved away from Kilgard and our little yellow house was home no more. She wasn't able to visit us often and my siblings had their own families to raise by then.

When Christmas season arrived our supervisors said we would go hunting for a tree up in the mountain behind the school. Eagerly I got a few friends together and we set out to cut a tree, one just for us. We found one but of course we did not have a saw or tool to cut it down. Not wanting to wait for our supervisors, we decided to get it down and off the mountain. We all climbed on one side of it and swung and pulled until it gave and broke. Off we went carrying our treasured tree and singing *O Christmas Tree...* when, out of nowhere, Miss C. appeared! Boy was she angry with us for going up on our own! Of course I was the culprit, so I got the brunt of her anger. She took our tree away. I thought we would not be allowed to put it up but she gave it back a few days later. We made decorations and sang songs. It was good with Miss C. and Miss R., and if only we were not in the school I could have enjoyed being with these two kind ladies whole-heartedly. Increasingly, I only had a great desire to get the hell out of that school. The system that ruined so many children there was nothing that could make me feel that St. Mary's could replace home. It was still prison to me.

I eagerly went home for the summer with a plan to never go back to St. Mary's. My oldest sister said it was up to mom, and I wasn't living with her then. So I set out to go to my mom and have her see why I needed to stay home. I made promises, pleaded and nagged her. Finally mom said I could stay back only if I lived with my sister and behaved. I was ecstatic! I'm home! Well, I was at my sister's home in Chilliwack.

I was going to attend another St. Mary's – a Catholic day school. It didn't matter to me as long as I was not in residential school. I went there with my sister's children and many from local reserves. Although it wasn't residential it had many of the same rules. I did not progress academically there and just did my time, happy when three o'clock came, and I could catch the school bus home with my relatives.

I soon learned how white people felt about First Nations there! There was one incident in particular, when the school bus driver drove us all home. He would go way past our reserve houses, out into the farming area where the white kids lived, bypassing our stop which was right there on his route. Then we had to back track and walk a long road home. The following day I got up and called the kids to the front of the bus just before he got to my sister's house. In a loud menacing voice I said "Stop here and let us off! Why do you make us walk all the way back?!" He looked at me in shock but stopped right where I asked him to. From then on he stopped at my sister's house as I summoned the others forward. I don't believe I need to write much more about that school year at this time. I spent it being rebellious and avoiding authorities at all costs.

From there I was placed in a convent in North Vancouver and attended yet another Catholic school, St. Thomas Aquinas. Needless to say the nuns had many incidents with me and I with them. If anything, my rebellious attitude increased. It was there they approved having all my teeth out – although they did not need to be extracted. Early extraction led to severe physical and emotional difficulties. Surgeries to repair would cost me many thousands of dollars and horrid pain.

It was a year filled with pain, some laughter, new friends and more. I was so happy my Mission residential school friend Marie was in the convent with me. She was still doing well then and was obedient with the nuns. We carried on right where we left off, she trying to get me to listen to the nuns and me not listening. We both stayed for the full school year. Marie was very serious with her boyfriend and went home to marry him at the tender age of fifteen. I went back to my sister's house in Chilliwack.

Chapter Twelve

In A Nutshell:
What Happened After Residential School?

"Female Leaders"

For several years I became lost, not knowing or valuing who I was. My journey was bumpy, sad, joyful and full of what I called celebrating freedom, or doing as I pleased. I lived a short time with my sisters and soon had a son. I was a single struggling mother on social assistance. I did menial jobs unhappily and got married young, thinking my life would improve. It did not.

After my young years of not moving ahead I decided to do something with my life. Finally fed up with continual struggles and hurdles I sought a way out. I realized the only way for me to succeed was through education. That was the beginning of another chapter in my life.

After much work and many hardships I did succeed academically. For a few years I lost my Indian Status when I married a non-native man. Because of that, I could not receive support of any kind from my Sumas First Nation Band according to the Indian Act. So I paid for my own schooling costs. I went through an upgrading process then on to college, then to the University of British Columbia. This meant working while I studied, even while I attended UBC and earned my education degrees. I look back on that challenging climb with pride. It made me work hard to get where I want to be and to appreciate all that I have, physically, emotionally, mentally and spiritually. I became a public school teacher, school principal, a public school district administrator and Chief of my Band.

There is too much to share about my life. My good friend, my former professor, an accomplished author and my confidant, Dr. Verna Kirkness said to me, "Remember you are only writing about your residential school experience." She said,

"Don't attempt to write your life story in this one! You will be writing volumes, Bea!" She is correct! I will save that for another time. Perhaps another book!

Presently I'm semi-retired but I remain active. I enjoy going into schools and talking to students and teachers. It was my engagement with the Abbotsford School District which inspired me to write this book. The District Aboriginal Principal, Darlene McDonald, brought me in to the schools to share my experience at Indian Residential School. My work with teachers Allison and Taryn resulted in twenty paintings created by their students, depicting detail from my story.

I plan to continue my work with school teachers, students and other organizations keen on learning First Nations history. I believe that is what Truth and Reconciliation is about. Working together; understanding each other; and accomplishing together on equal ground.

I had an elder chief say to me once, "If you leaders stood together in true unity, holding hands, you could make this building rise off the ground." I understand now what that National Chief meant so long ago. I totally believe that. We must put aside past battles, hurts, and anger, and join forces. We share this earth together. Let us cherish it while we can.

Afterword

By Dr. Tom Swanky, J.D.

"The Honey Apple"

Readers of Bea's story naturally will wonder how it came about that children from her community routinely found themselves at residential schools. Given the great disproportion between the harms and benefits, did the ancestors somehow fail their children?

Parents did resist the removal of their children to the schools. They repeatedly shielded them from the Indian agent, the police or the priests, case by case and time by time. Yet, as institutions, these schools processed children for several generations. Understanding how all this evolved for Sto:lo children requires a brief introduction to British colonialism in the North Pacific. Colonialism both weakened native households and gave rise to the residential schools as they came to be: instruments of what Canada officially acknowledges as a form of genocide.

Colonialism began in the North Pacific with the Oregon Treaty of 1846. The British and American empires used this treaty to divide their regional interests along the 49th parallel. Nowhere did they consult the original Peoples in this process. This arbitrary border separated the Sto:lo haphazardly and without their consent, some to become subjected to British rule and some to the Americans. And so children from Bea's community eventually would attend Canadian rather than American residential schools.

After the Oregon Treaty, British colonizers set out to dis-establish the existing systems of law, government and resource allocation while seating the Crown as a new sovereign power in their stead. To aid this over-throw, the colonizers promised any non-indigenous newcomers that they would have easy access to land and minerals. This carried with it an implicit promise that the colonizers would guarantee the newcomers immunity from the existing laws and the long-established sovereign authorities in the territories where they settled. In other words, while the original peoples almost universally respected the host/guest relationship, the colonizers invited newcomers to violate these norms. This laid a foundation of bad faith from which the non-indigenous community still has not recovered.

Sovereignty has two aspects: a grant of legitimate authority from the citizens to be governed and the physical power to make the laws effective. The colonizers made no attempt at avoiding conflict by gaining some grant of legitimate authority through negotiating treaties with the established authorities. This might have provided an orderly evolution to some form of shared sovereignty. Canadians are no strangers to such systems. Instead, the colonizers relied on violence, intimidation and fraud to marginalize and then displace the existing authorities. As a consequence, the Crown never gained any grant of legitimate authority as it gained the physical power to assert control over the original People in new territories.

Lacking grants of legitimate authority from the original Peoples over whom and in whose territories they would assume a right to govern, the colonizers based the Crown's right of sovereignty partly on the dishonorable principle that might is right and partly on a form of ethnocentrism. Nineteenth Century British ethnocentrism, and in its wake Canadian ethnocentrism, led the colonizers to an intemperate belief in the inherent superiority of their community and culture. This led to some excesses of cultural chauvinism and the degradation of all others as inferior, especially the original Peoples.

Cultural chauvinism saw the colonizers impose all manner of British institutions and radically violate the existing laws to impose new systems without consultation or compensation while ignoring the Crown's own policies as provided in the Royal Proclamation of 1763. As Elders in diverse communities describe it the degradation that accompanied colonialism in the North Pacific usually began with a rapid population loss, often through the criminal creation of "man-made" smallpox epidemics or by starvation as the most fertile land was seized for European-style agriculture to benefit the newcomers. A further loss of well-being came with being forced from their homes onto small "reserves." The degradation continued with the punishment of native authorities for continuing to apply the established laws and with the outlawing of potlatches, spirit dances, social gatherings and public meetings, except those in Christian churches. Residential schools were introduced to complete the elimination of the original Peoples as a distinct society by breaking the transmission of culture to native children while installing a new culture, as though they were mechanical - rather than human - beings.

In Sto:lo territory, this transition began with the gold rush of 1857/58. In these years, miners swarmed the territory and violently pushed the People from any location they desired. Most of these newcomers originated from California where miner militias often slaughtered the original Peoples at will. In effect, conditions for the Fraser River gold rush became an extension of those in California that scholars now recognize as having instituted a period of genocide.

This wave of newcomers to Sto:lo territory produced the "Fraser River Settlements." These settlements were a chain of non-indigenous communities stretching along the Fraser River through Sto:lo territory to Lillooet. Through the violence directed against the original Peoples during the gold rush, these Settlements became the first places where the Crown would achieve control on the ground in the mainland Colony of British Columbia.

The violence of the gold rush and the establishment of the Fraser River Settlements saw both a loss of absolute and relative numbers for the Sto:lo. A communities' number affects its ability to project the political presence necessary for physical control. As the Sto:lo and their land became increasingly subject to the will of officials appointed by a foreign power, the Sto:lo had less and less voice in the legislation or public administration of their territories. Even though the old laws and constitutions had not been repealed or transcended by the rule of law, they had increasingly less influence on the daily activity of those now living in Sto:lo territory. Not only is there the loss of influence on public policy even within one's own society, there is also a recognition that those with power are little interested in hearing from the subjugated People, unless their voices can be heard as supportive of the occupation. The Sto:lo experience was not unique. In losing their political power, the original Peoples in each territory soon also lost the privilege of educating their children or even influencing their schooling.

Any People undergoing occupation by a foreign power will experience depression, despair and behaviours common to those enduring traumatic events. The occupation of Sto:lo territory was brutal, uncompromising and devastating. While hope fueled the colonizers and newcomers, indigenous communities were forced to cope with a series of traumatic events on such a scale that the effect is virtually incomprehensible at an individual level. Individuals, and individual families with children, became isolated from one another and often even from their own sense of self in the multi-faceted assault of colonialism: displacement of many kinds, forcible removal of children, denial of identity, aggressive assimilation strategies causing mental harm, racial discrimination, extra-judicial restriction of movements and violence perpetrated by settlers or their police force. Modern waves of assimilation policies still produce trauma leading to despair, grieving, hopelessness and even suicide.

Marginalization brought dispossession and poverty. As the original Peoples increasingly lost access to their land, they lost their self-sufficiency. Instead of citizens cooperating with each other essentially as equals, the opportunities available to the original Peoples were now only as servants and labourers in the employ of non-indigenous land owners or entrepreneurs operating under an entirely new social system. Nor is it psychologically a simple matter for any dispossessed People to see their resources used without consent or compensation and, in this case, without even acquiring some colour of "aboriginal title" as understood in British law.

People desperate simply to feed their children necessarily give other concerns less attention, such as the best education for their children. This brought in other considerations. The original Peoples placed a very high value on education. Each succeeding generation in oral cultures must become a repository for a People's entire body of knowledge. Native children were learning constantly from the Elders and at potlatches or story times. In addition, the original Peoples universally respected religious or spiritual figures. And it had been Catholic priests who established the first non-indigenous schooling in Sto:lo territory. The original Peoples were not fools. They recognized the advantages in technological innovations brought by the newcomers. They were led to believe that the residential schools would be a gateway for their children to master this new age. Some ancestors, especially in the beginning, considered the risk worthwhile and were inclined to accept the priests' reassurances. Before the residential schools became mandatory, children briefly did have a more balanced opportunity for learning in both worlds. It was possible to see the outline of a trail to better days.

Unfortunately the trust placed in non-indigenous authority figures was betrayed. The best hopes of the ancestors were not realized. The Truth and Reconciliation Commission documented this part of the larger tragedy brought by colonialism at length. In the meantime, a lingering colonial ethnocentrism has seen the curators and academic gatekeepers of British Columbia's history continue to insulate the general public from the Elders' teaching concerning instances of genocide and inhumane suffering. The findings of the Truth and Reconciliation Commission were a critical break with this tradition. The initiatives pursued by the Abbotsford and other British Columbia school districts that now sees Elders like Bea sharing their experiences and those of their community are an important part of continuing the break and passing this torch of truth-telling and memory.

Dr. Swanky is the author of several books. His most recent work is The Smallpox War in Nuxalk Territory. *He also has written a general introduction to the 1862 smallpox epidemics,* The True Story of Canada's "War" of Extermination on the Pacific.

Author's Note

Truth And Reconciliation

"Principal"

Indian Residential Schools were in operation from the 1860s to 1996 in Canada. After much damage and destruction, Indigenous people stepped up and began taking control of the terrible situation that resulted from the residential school impact. The genocidal effects reach far and wide. Many children died in those schools and many died after, leading desolate tragic lives as a result of residential schools' effects.

In the 1980s residential schools began phasing out. In 1996 the last residential school was shut down for good.

There began the movement of the people. Residential school survivors began speaking out about the traumatic abuse they endured. Leaders confronted the federal government, naming the religious orders who worked with federal government leaders to callously remove children from parents in the early nineteen hundreds and some as early as the late 1800s. After much publicity, meetings, forums and court cases, the federal government acted. Prime Minister Stephen Harper made a public apology to Indigenous people.

In 2016 the government invited survivors from across the country to Ottawa to witness the Truth and Reconciliation Commissioners' report resulting from years of research, including hearings of residential school survivors. I was one of the chosen survivors to attend the fully paid event along with two of my sisters Frieda and Dianna. Three Survivors from Bella Coola attended also – Caroline Mack, Wally Webber, and William Nelson. Caroline Mack is a respected Nuxalk Elder who is 81 years "young." She was a joy to be with in Ottawa, keeping us laughing as she went off determined to see the Parliament buildings, museums, and more. We often had to go find her - she moves fast! Wally Webber is a Nuxalk

Chief elected in the Band Council and he is also a Hereditary Chief. He proudly joined us at dinners and gatherings, as well as being our captain and guard as we roamed around!

There were thousands of people moving about, dancing, singing and talking. It was an exciting and hopeful time for us all. Many Indigenous people affected by that system travelled of their own accord. One determined survivor chosen to attend was afraid of flying, so she drove from Vancouver Island all the way to Ottawa, from West Coast close to East Coast! The huge announcements were so important for healing. The government stated that the Truth and Reconciliation Commission was a major priority for them and declared it a major goal of all government Ministries. I was so excited!

Ottawa was booming with happy, encouraged, hopeful Indigenous people, visiting there from coast to coast to coast! All government parties were present at the release of the report, and many elected chiefs were visible, but it was the Survivors who had a tremendous impact. The Honourable Murray Sinclair, Chair of the Commission, made an astounding televised report to us all as we sat in anticipation and excitement. He reported many findings but, in short, he said with conviction that the Commissioners' report found the Indian Residential Schools' actions, attitudes, and treatment of children was NO LESS THAN GENOCIDE! He said the schools were a clear, purposeful act to destroy who the Indigenous Peoples are, their values, their entire system and, in doing so, their pride. I shouted out in agreement as we all did, clapping and dancing in the excitement of witnessing the authorities' recognition of what governments and churches did to us. An unconscionable heinous crime. It would take generations to mend, heal and build up again! Unity among

the people, especially us survivors, was steadfast and comforting. We felt understood and appreciated at long last!

After the shocking reports from the commissioners, Justin
Trudeau, who was not yet in the running for Prime Minister,
gave passionate speeches and flourishing overtures to all of
us there. He promised honest changes for the progress of my
people. He wept at the stories he heard. I wondered at his sin-
cerity. All politicians present had their say. So few do I believe in. The connections I made with myself and others,
however, overrode any doubting disparaging thoughts I had
then. There was much feasting, dancing, exciting chatter and
gatherings among us in those three days!

Although I was happy that "truth" and "reconciliation"
were promised, and I felt this exhilaration racing up inside
me, it was muddled by a foreboding apprehension. Like when
I was finally allowed to go home to my family, my village; I
was overjoyed, but wondered what I would face when I got
home. My family security was no more, my reserve changed,
my people changed and life as I knew it was changed. However, the final outcome was that I was home at last. Was it
freedom I sought or more than that? Only time would tell.

I see clearly that Truth and Reconciliation is not what we
hoped it would be, not yet.

Indigenous Peoples are expected to reconcile with governments and corporations. Governments and corporations do
not reconcile with Indigenous Peoples. They say they consult
with our Bands but do not. They talk to a few elected Indian
Affairs chiefs but not with the people. They call that consulting. Which they believe is enough to move on with their
agendas of mining, oil pipelines and more.

"Truth and Reconciliation" therefore, is one sided, unbalanced, and without truth. The federal government often joins forces with giant corporations and go ahead with earth shattering destructive movements despite First Nations opposition. They at times visit an elder to talk of wonderful beneficial projects and call that consulting; they're respecting elders whom they think can be fooled. One day some suits came to visit my older brother Dr. Ray Silver, once an active elder of our community, who was working in his garden despite near blindness. They spoke of beautiful plans and what their money could do for our reserves. He listened respectfully as he went on weeding, then he stood up, facing them squarely, he pulled out his only money in his pocket, a five dollar bill and said, "Here take this, when their no more food left here, eat that." Well they went on their way finding him very rude. We laughed hard at this and so many people appreciated his forthright response. Good on Ray; he is known for telling it like it is, even if it is a harsh bare truth.

The majority of Indigenous Peoples did not make an agreement with Kinder Morgan pipelines. But Prime Minister Trudeau did. He bought those destructive pipelines for billions of dollars! The majority of Indigenous people are opposed to his actions. This is not the truth and reconciliation that he promised his government would follow diligently. All those heart felt passionate speeches made to residential school survivors. Trudeau claimed to want to rectify the Indigenous situation in many ways. But did he imagine that could erase the many abuses imposed on Indigenous people in the past? Doing what he is doing to my people now is no less than bestowing colonization upon us again! It continues on many levels.

We have a long way to go in honestly practicing truth and reconciliation in this country. Before reconciliation can truly happen the harshness of the naked truths must be appreciated by the governments and whole heartedly condemned for what they are. Having said that, I appreciate what the Commission into Indian Residential Schools brought forth. It brought out the astounding sad facts of what residential school did to our families and our communities for generations and generations. The world knows of the genocide committed upon us now. It was hidden and denied too long. It rests in our hands now, to deal with as we think best. That is what I am doing today. I pray that our leaders will do all that is necessary politically so our precious children may have good lives, better lives than I and thousands of our ancestors endured in residential schools.

Amid all this challenging muddle that surrounds me, I carry on with life as we all do. My years in residential school, I believe, were meant to be a part of my journey that guided me onto this winding path I am on now. All that I experienced good and bad was for a reason. Fortunately after many hurdles, ups and downs, I have come to the realization that my hatred of the governments, churches and those who hurt and damaged me is yet another trauma to overcome. I only hurt myself by hating. And they are the ones that taught me hatred. Throughout this rocky journey of life, I learned it is best to forgive and carry on in a good way. I can forgive those people but I shall never forget. I cannot forget the abuse and the horrors I experienced and witnessed. I have put those away on a secret shelf and take some of them out occasionally when I need to look at a lesson those experiences taught me. Examine, think, cherish and go forward. It is all a part of me.

Today I love who I have become, prickly thorns and all. I love myself and I love life.

I will continue to work for the betterment of our children and families' situations and I will still go to battle when required, of course choosing those battles wisely. My people deserve a good life on this earth. I deserve a good life on this earth also. I pray we can all work together to make our earth a better place as she provides life for all of us here: red, black, yellow and white, we are all brothers and sisters. Once we are united we can make our world a better place.

All My Relations

Bea Silver

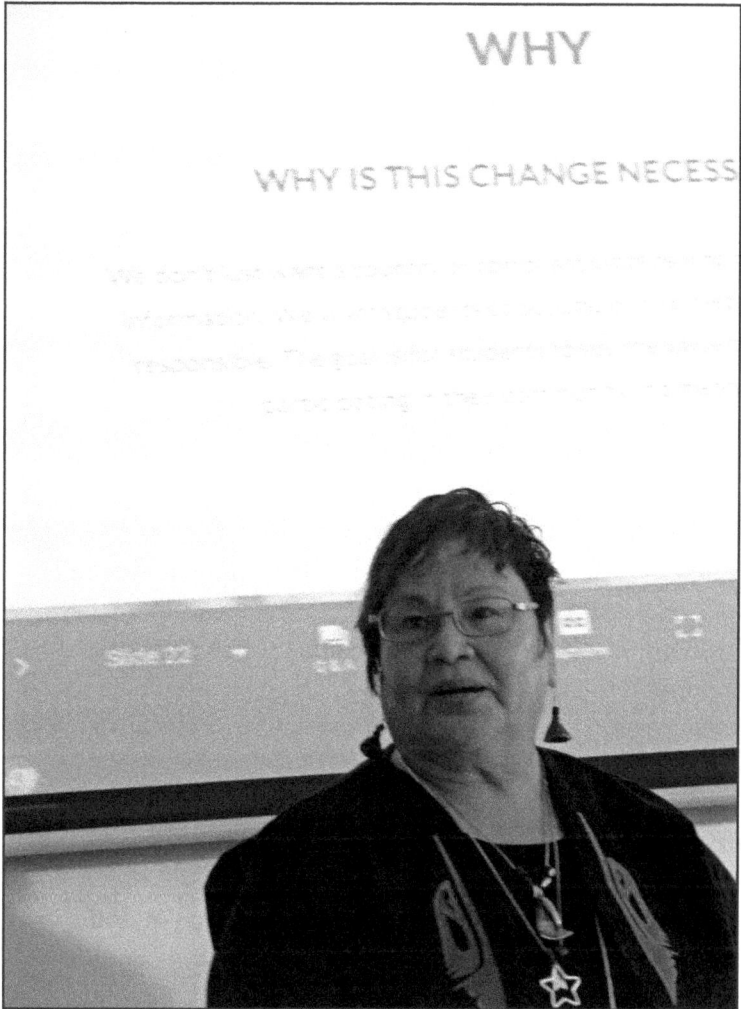

*Beatrice Silver at a reconciliation event in education,
October 21, 2018, at Abbotsford Senior Secondary.*

Acknowledgments

My Mama, my mentor, my hero: Jean (MaryJane Silver), deserves whole hearted acknowledgement for who I am today. Her unconditional love and support throughout my growing years is the foundation of my being.

The following people inspired and supported me throughout the undertaking of many challenges I faced writing the story of my residential school years.

My Nuxalk husband Peter Tallio nurtured that seed within me to talk, write and heal from traumas of residential school. Traumas I carried on through tumultuous chapters of my life. And they were many.

Dr. Ray Silver, my brother, humbly and lovingly spread his knowledge without hesitation when asked to. He spent much time in Abbotsford school district, universities and numerous agencies and corporations. He shared our history and his beliefs concerning our environment. He encouraged and supported my endeavours to complete education degrees and keep going when obstacles caused me to stumble and at times to fall. Ray was there for me. Later his daughter Bernice Silver Graham stepped in when, sadly, he passed last year. She excitedly supported and encouraged me as I wrote and reached out to many people.

My sisters Mona, Dianna, Frieda and Von had some anxiety concerning this difficult project. Mona said to me, "you can write it all!.. all that I told you!" I did that.

My brother Herman's daughters, especially Jackie and Charlotte, faithfully followed the work I was doing from the beginning, cheering me onward.

For Abbotsford School District, I put my hands way up: for Darlene MacDonald, District Principal of Indigenous Education, and her teacher daughter Taryn MacDonald and colleague Alexandra Klassen. They had an idea to work with me on my residential school experiences and have the Robert Bateman Secondary School's Art Activism students depict my story through paintings. There began wonderful lifelong relationships and a very worthy project which you see in this book.

Thank you very much to the students who have allowed their work to be included here. Thanks to them for sharing their time and energy and creativity with my story.

Dr. Verna Kirkness my professor my mentor and my dear friend. She inspired me throughout my UBC education and often with my personal life. Verna said to me, "be sure to include some of your humour in your writing. Most of these stories are so sad. Be yourself when you write." Well, Verna some of those pieces of being myself had to be deleted. However, I did attempt to be me, Bea Silver.

Tom Swanky wrote the very knowledgeable Afterword for my story. Tom talked to me throughout the year of my work as I sometimes struggled and wept discussing what I was writing and who I talked to that day. He put up with hearing how I was feeling, cuss words and all.

Kerry Coast is an awesome publisher who believed in me when I did not think I could write much more of my experiences in St Mary's school.

Finally, and with much love and respect, I acknowledge

the students – my friends from St. Mary's residential school who I shared with, cried with, and laughed with. Without you, my story would have been filled with fake names. Thank you for allowing me to print your names and snippets of our time together.

Norman Patrick Ike Silver
Maureen Saul Wehey
Rhoda Peters
Charlene Ned
Melvin Williams
John Kelly, twin- Hugh Kelly (d)
Norma Anderson Nahanee
Norma Francis
Yvonne Francis Tumundhey
Wanda Charlie Stogan
Ann Smith and Mary Smith, for allowing me to tell a bit of Kate and Bradley's story.
Nina Charlie, for allowing me to tell a bit about her mother Marie.

I thank all of the people from Sumas First Nation, Abbotsford, my home, for coming forth and supporting me in this healing project. My family, my people, my home:
Thank you.

Stories for Art Activism

Transcriptions
of Bea's presentations
to the Art Activism class

"Chief"

*The following stories are presented here
just as they were transcribed from classroom
recordings.*

*These stories were related to students in the
Art Activism class amidst many hours and days,
over weeks and months of interaction between students, teachers, and their guest, Bea Silver.
Students spent more than just class time on these
paintings, coming in after school and even on
weekends to complete them.*

*The development of this book was made easier
by telling the stories to those wonderful students,
and they share a special part in the recalling and
retelling of a very difficult experience.*

*Perhaps this is a small part of what we mean by
"reconciliation."*

The story of
The Boy
and the Honey Apple

There were just a few of us
that were left home when I
was younger, because all of
the kids were taken to the
residential school. I would
go down the hill to see Sid at
his farm and follow him as he collected up the cows.

He couldn't even be bothered with me, I was a nui-
sance to him. I followed behind him, and he had a whip that
he gathered the cows with. I thought that it was a really important job so I got a stick and went along with him.

There was a huge apple tree there. I saw these apples
and I said, "I really I want an apple," so he went up the tree
and got me one.

Have you ever seen an apple with honey in it? You
could see this white clear spot in the apple skin that looks
like water is squished into it.

I asked, "What is this?" He answered, "It's honey, eat
it!" and he kept on his way and left me behind.

He was really quiet, and I never got to know him. He
didn't go to residential school and I didn't get to return
home until I left school. Then when I left school, I left
everything.

The story of the
Indian Affairs Nurse

When the Indian agent came, and he often did, I remember my parents and the other people in the village would be dashing about, not really wanting to be examined or questioned, or have their homes inspected by this Indian agent, but there he was. The nurse, one time, came puffing up with her little case of needles to give us shots. My dad was alone, my mom was always home but that day she wasn't and so he very humbly and very meekly complied with the nurse's wishes to: "Get the kids and get them over here."

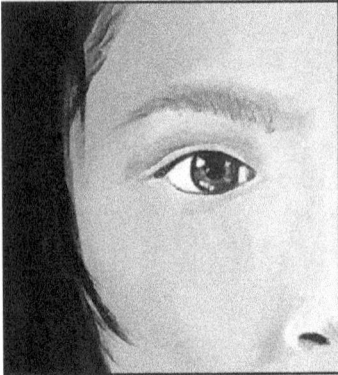

The other kids rolled up their sleeves to get their needles but I wouldn't. I ran in circles and refused, and said some angry words. I took my little brother, who was about two or three, and we went under the house. I remember looking out and all I could see was the nurse's big bosom as she was bending over.

"Come on children now, it won't hurt," she shouted under the porch.

I swore at her, and told her to go to hell. My dad was mortified! Remember, I was raised with big brothers, and so sometimes I talk like my big brothers, which isn't always very nice.

She finally had to give up and leave us, but we stayed under the house longer because I knew we would get it when we came out: my dad would be really angry because we embarrassed him.

We had those kinds of people coming in to do stuff with us… and they would take us away, too.

The story of
The Doll

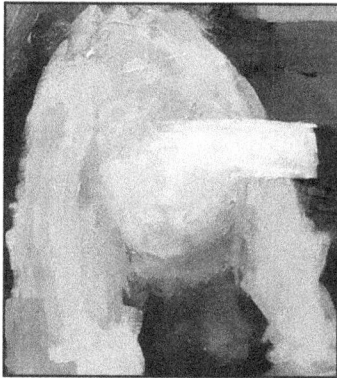

When non-natives came to our door it was always my mom who went to the door because she wasn't native. My dad was really meek. One day he saw me playing with this little girl, her parents owned the store on the reserve. She had a baby buggy and I didn't have such things, so I was happily playing with her.

You don't know the difference, you don't look at colors, you don't notice race as a child. Not unless someone tells you. My dad said, "You're not to play with her anymore, she's a white girl and they don't like us. You're not to play with her, you come home and don't do that again."

When I went to residential school, all I got was that we were inferior and that we weren't as good as others – that there were things wrong with us – but I always fought that.

The story of my **Brothers Boxing**

I had my mom, I had my older sisters. I had my brothers, and they all had very strong personalities. My brothers were kind of wild: fighters, drinkers, and loggers.

They taught me to be tough. They even taught us to box; all of the sisters would have to box. I was telling my husband about this once, and he asked, "Why do you think they did that? They were all boxers too." I said, "I think, now, they did that so we would be tough every-which-way." Their way was to be tough, that kind of physical tough, but my way is to be emotionally and mentally tough. My mom had endured so much without sticking up for herself, and I always told myself that I wasn't going to be that way. I was going to speak out.

The story of
Where is My Brother?

My oldest brother Ray used to come as a guest speaker to this school district all the time until he passed away last year. He would tell his story about residential school.

He went to Port Alberni with his brother, who was a bit younger than him. They had a worse story. They went to school in the 1930s. His brother was my brother, too, but I didn't know him: Dolton. He died there.

We still don't know how he died, it's a mystery to us. They sent my brother home, and the priest told them, "You have to go home by a ferry in Port Alberni."

He asked, "Where's my brother Dolton?" He told me

that the priest said, "He's downstairs in a coffin." "He was in a box. A wooden box," my brother said. That was all they told him.

Nobody knows how Dolton died. My parents didn't know, my brother didn't know. They just sent him home.

Beatrice Elaine Silver

The story of my
First Arrival

I went to St Mary's Residential School in Mission when I was seven years old. There was much abuse; we weren't allowed to speak our language; and we were not allowed to practice our culture. We were totally divided from our siblings, and from each other. When I first went to school, I was so happy because I'd be seeing my big sisters. Nobody told me what would happen. We were separated. I was taken in alone and we were stripped of our clothes. We were put in the dungeon part of the school where they had shower stalls and that's where they thought they needed to cleanse us of lice or whatever we might have, and I assure you we didn't... but they poured disinfectant on us and it stung! Little girls were jumping around and crying.

It was so shocking to go for my humble little home on the reserve, with my mom who I love dearly, into that atmosphere. We never saw our clothes again, they were taken. Anything the kids came with was all taken. We were put into their clothing and our hair was cut off.

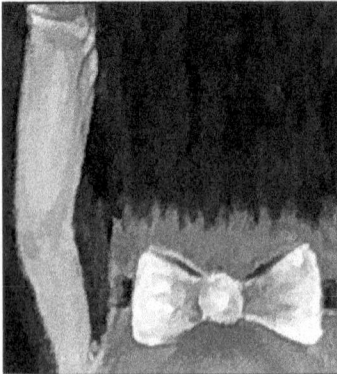

The story of my
First Communion

When I was in grade one, they started training us on the grounds of religion. Catholic religion was the foundation of the school environment, and that was a shock. Making your first communion was a huge thing, and they trained us early on to get ready for the communion. We would have a pretty white dress. Mine wasn't that fancy, not like some of the other little girls' dresses, because my family was really poor. We didn't have access to pretty dresses or money.

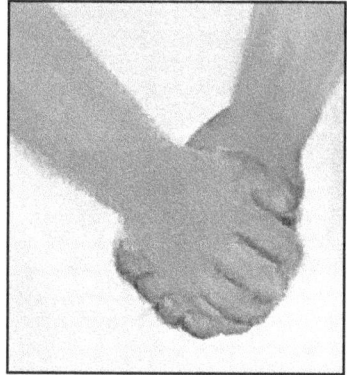

My dad logged when he could; he left the reserve to go logging. He got some money together and had my older sister go buy some material to make some kind of pretty dress for my first communion. On the day, I was getting more and more worried as I waited for this dress. Priscilla came along in a beautiful organza dress, it had those fake sleeves you can put on or take off, all lacey, and her veil... I talked to her about that recently.

She said "I remember that, and I want to thank you."

I asked her, "Why?"

She said, "Because you were so nice to me, and the other girls were really mean because I had beautiful clothes, and they didn't."

I didn't have a veil, they gave me this ancient one from one hundred years before that some little girl must have worn. My dad had bought me white shoes.

For that one day, we felt good when we made our first communion. We had the white dresses they gave us, little pretty pictures of the blessed virgin, and a little white bible. That was our special day.

The story of
The Cafeteria

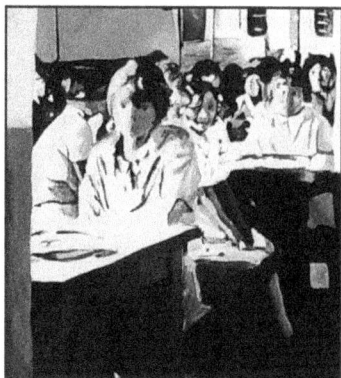

We used to eat in a kind of dungeon at the old school. When we first went there they had a basement and it was all cement. We all lined up and we never saw our brothers or any of the boys because they were at the other end of the dungeon. If we didn't eat our breakfast, whether it be bread, porridge, or the meal from the night before, or two weeks before, they didn't care, they put it all back into a big pot and served it to us again and again and again.

I wouldn't eat it. I learned to make food unimportant.

Other kids talk about being starving, and they were! They were starving. One boy was in the cafeteria and was sneaking out peanut butter on a piece of paper. The priest wasn't going to tolerate that, so he took him into the middle of the cafeteria, the dungeon where we ate, and strapped him until his hands bled.

All this for wanting to take out peanut butter because he was hungry. They didn't feed us much, we didn't get snacks or anything. All of these kinds of things happened. People kind of look at us in disbelief because our stories are so unbelievable, and that's why a lot of us would never tell our stories.

The story of becoming a
Teacher

When I went home from school, my dad had died. My mom had started drinking for awhile because we were gone, and then my dad was dead. That's the period where I didn't really know who I was, and really had trouble finding my way.

Many yars later, when I had my little boy and was living in Chilliwack, I decided I didn't want to be a single mom on welfare. I didn't want that kind of life, and there started my hard work, going back to school to get an education. Education is expensive, and I was lucky to get bursaries here and there, but I basically went on loans. I also had a little boy, but I went right through to get my degree.

I started teaching in 1981. I only had nine native kids. Most of them were quiet... they were really quiet and shy. My first goal was to work on collaboration, to work on acceptance with everybody. Because those kids are coming to you, like we do, with personalities and a wealth of knowledge, with a lot of experiences.

That's what they didn't recognize or recognize when we went into residential school. To me, it's really important that we acknowledge, recognize, accept, and embrace.

The story of
Bradley and Kate

The school held a lot of sadness. A lot of bad things went on there. Kids died there.

I asked this one boy where my friend's little brother went. I asked, "Do you know anything that could have happened to Bradley?"

He said, "No, I just remember them carrying his body out in the middle of the night. We don't know how Bradley died."

When I talked to his sister, she said the priest got in touch with her parents and her grandfather. They were going to bury Bradley in the graveyard where our playground was. She said that her grandfather got a car together and went to get his little body. He was in grade four, I remember that. They took him home to Mount Currie.

That was the first one that I knew of that died there. More died. There were the girls, when I was in school, who died there; young senior girls.

Bradley had a sister named Kate. When we would run away, she would come. And now we all know why she came: to look after us. She was big and husky and wore blue jeans that were rolled up. She was just really a toughie. She was an amazing girl. To me, she was a big girl but, at that time, she would have been maybe fourteen. She used to look out for us.

We did that for each other, a lot of us.

The story of
Don't Tell

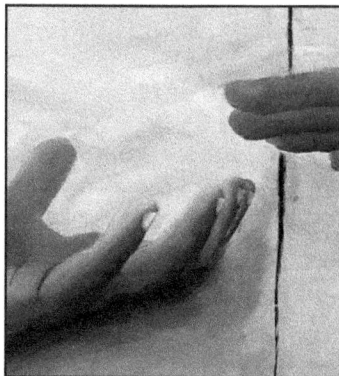

There was mystery surround-
ing our residential school,
and I think that a lot of our
children were sexually
abused. It was quite common
to see them being taken from
their beds at night, taken out
of the dorm and brought
somewhere else.

    I have a really close
friend, Maureen Colormall. I
said to her, "Do you remember, Maureen, when we used to
push our beds together in that dormitory in the cubicle? Six
of us to beds. You told me you were having really bad
nightmares. Do you remember?" and she said, "I do. Somebody kept pressing on me, all this pressure was on me."

    "What do you think that was Maureen?" And she said,
"I don't know."

    I said, "Do you remember when we put our beds to-
gether because there were three on one side and three on
the other?"

    She sis, and I asked further, "And do you remember
when I woke up and I told you something happened to me
but I don't know what?"

    She said, "No, I do not remember."

We put a lot out of our heads.

    Some of the girls would tell me, "I don't remember, I

don't want to remember so don't discuss it with me." So, I don't. I respect that. And when things like that happened you didn't tell. You just didn't tell and lots of kids today won't tell.

I say, "Tell."
Yell it out.
Tell others what happened.

The story of
The Orchard

We had one day out of the whole year where they did something nice for us. They brought us, along with a whole bunch of orphans, to Birch Bay. It was a big thing we looked forward to for June, before we went home (those who got to go home).

It happened that I was allowed out with some other kids and my sister for the weekend but we had to be back at a certain time.

We were rarely ever allowed home, and we got back to the residential school late. It wasn't our fault, it was who-ever was driving us back. So they held us back and punished us. We weren't allowed to go to the Birch Bay event, where they had the playground and the Ferris Wheel and all those things. I said to my sister and the others that were kept back, "Let's go to the orchard!"

The old school had an orchard. We didn't get the fruit off that orchard. We weren't even allowed in that orchard. It had cherries and plums and apples and everything, and being June the cherries were out, so I said "let's go to the orchard."

So we ran. They were scared but I wasn't. Away we went to the orchard across the field and we ate cherries and had a great time. Then we saw the horses. I got on a horse! I climbed on the fence and I jumped on the horse and I flew around the orchard. The kids were really scared.

"You're gonna fall off!" they said.

But I flew along on that horse. I would run away to the orchard alone sometimes after that to get on one of those horses and ride. To me, it was freedom.

The story of going
Home

When I began going home I would be so excited. More and more though, my home was becoming unfamiliar. They taught us to be ashamed of who we were. They taught us to be ashamed of our reserve and of our parents and how we believed and how we lived. When I came home, for the first while it was good. I wanted to be home, and I couldn't wait to see my mom.

I was more close to my mom because my dad was strict, and he drank a lot. More and more, "home" became stranger and stranger. I came home to a house where the whole village didn't have children anymore. The whole reserve got depressed, and drinking became an issue.

It was like an empty nest, but the whole village was that way; every village.

Quite often I hear my classmates say, "I left and never went back," meaning they had left the school and the reserve and never went back.

You become lost if you don't know your roots. You become lost if you don't know who you are. If you don't have that foundation, you become lost out on the streets. That's when you can become lost to drink or drugs. You don't know how to rear your children or raise your families.

That is what we're battling today, with a lot of our people. That was life; we became strangers in our own homes and to our parents. It was like we didn't know them anymore and we didn't know our siblings; our brothers and sisters anymore.

Because we weren't allowed to know them in school.

The story of how
You Could Write

My story isn't doom and gloom. As I said before, everything happens for a reason and it's all about lessons in life. If you asked me if I would do it all again, I'd say yes. It made me who I am, and I'm proud of who I am today.

It wasn't an easy journey, but there were some joyful moments with my friends. That, to me, was really important. To have the friends with me, and I have to say that the best times were with the kids that I grew up with.

I was always rebellious, but there was this one little nun - she was the sweetest little thing - and for whatever reason she took me under her wing. She realized I could read anything. She would give me everything and I would read it.

She always told me I could write. "You could be a writer! You could go places... but you don't listen... you don't behave."

I think now, that's how I was when I was a little girl.

The story of becoming
Principal

I started my Masters in Administration because I feel I'm a good leader. I had my own ideas of how education could be, and I wanted to practice that. I left here and went to teach in Bella Coola.

I taught Special Education and that's where I became principal. I did come home, and worked for the ministry of education. I oversaw the whole Fraser Valley for Aboriginal Education, and that year decided I would run for Chief.

The thing I had was determination.

It's like that old song, "I did it my way... took a long time but I did it."

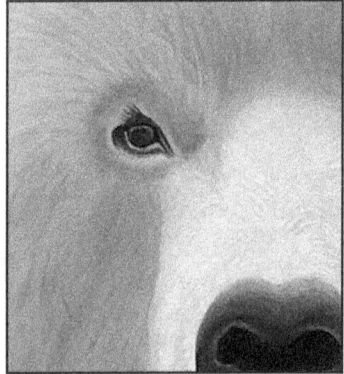

The story of becoming
Chief

The mining companies on Sumas Mountain had free reign. They're still doing it... but to make a long story short, I shut them down. I blocked the road. I worked closely with your mayor then, Mary Reeves. I was friends with Mary. She supported me in doing this, and it created a big kerfuffle across British Columbia.

I was out on the roads 24/7 to keep them blocked. Amidst this I sent a letter to all these rich corporations and said, "Come to our longhouse, and we will meet."

They came with their wives. I had the women of the reserve make a feast for them. They came in, not expecting that they would get welcomed like this, and we served them dinner.

I stood up and I said to them, "I'm not blocking the road because I'm angry with you. I'm not blocking the road or your mining companies to shut you down. I'm blocking the road because you're interfering with my people." I said, "we wake up to blasts, we wake up to trucks rolling through our reserve..." and so I talked on about why I was doing what I was doing: "I'm doing it because I want my people to have a better life."

So there began a relationship with the mining company

owners. We came to an agreement. They built sidewalks, they built a new road, that road is there today. Where they don't need to go through our reserve, they go through the mountain and down.

Reconciliation isn't just about land, and resources, and water, and fish, and all of that good stuff. It's about how we relate to each other, it's about working together, it's about respecting and acknowledging one another.

The story about
The TRC

Prime Minister Harper decided to choose a group of us from across Canada to go to Ottawa for a huge conference. It was quite an experience to hear all the stories. We got into groups and talked, shared, and cried. Commissioner Murray Sinclair gave a powerful speech that had everybody standing.

He said our history was not just abuse, it was genocide, what our children went through. He is also a former student of Indian residential school and now a senator. It was very powerful. Trudeau said that he would work with us and do what he could to reconcile. What it meant to him and our politicians was, say we want the money from our mine, or we want our fishing rights. Yes, that is important: we lost a lot and they are still mining our our lands - but to me it's deeper. It's so much deeper to accept us for who we are and respect us. If you go on to the lands near us and you're going to mine the hell out of the mountain, respect that we live below that mountain, and it was part of us. Work *with* us. That was my fight when I was Chief.

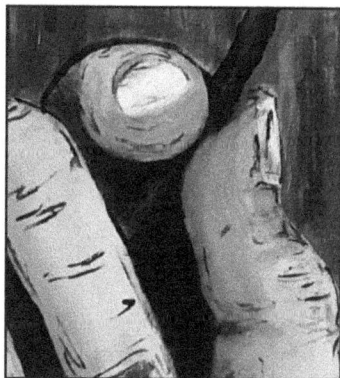

The story of
Ray

Ray was a giver and what he did, he did quietly. Right until he died he had the most beautiful garden on the reserve. An orchard, and raspberries... in this picture, he's in his orchard by an apple tree, and he's holding out an apple. This is so Ray. It's because of him I'm here doing what I'm doing. When I was a struggling student he'd give me $500 to help me through, because I paid my own way. He was our pillar; he was the foundation. For our family and for who I am today.

The story of
Female Leaders

I always used to say, at the Chief's table, that the people who will make a big change for our communities, and for our current situation, will be women.

I see all women with inner beauty and inner strength. The women are the ones that carry the baby, the ones that keep the house and the family together, and long ago, it was the woman who led the villages. They took care of the villagers, the man's job was to go out and provide.

All my life, I have seen strength in women. We are all leaders in some way. We all have a strength in us that we just search for, and find, because it's there.

It's in all of you.

Toq'we'ia

When I was very little my mother Jean Silver told me this story several times. I always begged her to tell it to me. Her calming voice and manner was soothing and I felt secure, so I often drifted off to sleep. She told it like this:

Now a long time ago, when there were lots of trees and animals all around and the mountains were thick with them, there lived a huge wild woman: Toq'we'ia. She survived up in the mountains with many wild vegetables, fish, and deer to eat. She also collected medicines from the earth to use for any kind of illness, so she remained healthy.

But there came a time when she wasn't satisfied with all she had. Toq'we'ia began thinking about the villages below the mountains. "I'm going down there to check on those people and see how they're living," she decided, and she trundled her Big, Hairy, Scary Self down, down, down the mountain.

Well, when she got down to the villages it was dark so she roamed from house to house peeking in windows. She just went poking about, all around the village. She watched the families: particularly the children. Toq'we'ia, being a no-nonsense woman, noticed when children weren't listening to parents and grandparents. "Hmmmm these little humans need to be taught to behave!" she thought, in her strict and purposeful manner. She took her Big, Hairy, Scary Self back up, up, up to her home in the mountain.

Toq'we'ia formed a plan. She decided to go back down to the village the next night and collect up all these kids who were naughty or went out at dark time. So that's what she did. The next night she thumped down the mountain to seek out naughty children.

Toq'we'ia took up a huge cedar basket she made specifically for collecting food, tied it on her back and began her journey down through thick trees and bushes. *Thump! Thump! Thump!* She dragged her basket over the rocks as she made her way down the mountain, thinking: "I'm going to have a feast of those children soon. Those that don't listen to their parents and those that play outside after dark!" and she greedily smacked her big chops. *Thump Thump! Thump!* She carried her Big, Hairy, Scary Self down-down-down that mountain.

She came to the village as it was nearing dusk. "Aha!" she cried, "there's some kids not inside as they should be!" And she easily scooped each one up into her huge basket, *clunk-smack-clunk* they each fell in – never mind how – they *plopped!* every-which-way on top of each other! She peeked inside some of the homes, seeing a few kids answering back and not wanting to go to bed. "I will scoop them up when they come outside in the dark. I will remember them," she chuckled, carrying her almost-filled basket. Toq'we'ia found a few more children and filled her big cedar basket. *Thump! Thump! Thump!* She dragged her heavy load and her Big, Hairy, Scary Self back home up-up-up the mountain.

She arrived and began tying up the children with cedar root twine as they cried and tried to get away. The wild woman made a huge fire. Carefully she began getting wild vegetables ready for her tasty feast. Now the kids were terrified and began talking among themselves. One big boy said, "she is collecting pitch for her fire and putting it on our eyes so we cannot see her. Close your eyes really tight, as tight as you can, when she puts it on your eyes. Then open your eyes when I say so." The children did that. The big wild woman began singing:

"Ooooooh my children, my tasty little yum-yums!
You deserve to be my feast
since yoooooouuuu don't listen!"
As she placed them around the fire with pitch on their eyes, they
were frightened but trusted their brother's plan would save them.
She put them in a circle around the fire, still gleefully singing. Then
the boy shouted: "Now open your eyes and charge at her. Now!"
The pitch popped off the children's eyes when they opened them,
and they could see Toq'we'ia poking the fire.

"Everyone push as hard as you can! Throw her in the fire!"
yelled their leader, and so they ran at her and they all push-push-
pushed her. Into the fire Toq'we'ia went! Right into the big fire she
fell screeching, "Oh my children! Don't hurt me. I love you all and
I will get you home!" She cried out and tried to escape the fire, but
they pushed and pushed some more. Her Big, Hairy, Scary Self
turned to ash in the giant bonfire she had made to roast the children.
She screeched and screeched and screeched until finally her cries
grew quieter and weaker, turning into annoying buzzing sounds as
she burned up. All the thick smoke from her Big, Hairy, Scary Self
turned into a cloud of mosquitoes buzzing away and all around.
The children happily went home together, vowing to forever listen
to moms-dads-grandparents-aunties-and-uncles. And so they did.

As for Toq'we'ia, her Big, Hairy, Scary Self became mosquitoes
that want your blood! Bat them away, they're only tiny bits of
Hairy, Scary Toq'we'ia. So children: listen to the adults who care
for you.

By
Mom Jean Silver
Kilgard, Sumas First Nation. Sto:lo

CPSIA information can be obtained
at www.ICGtesting.com
Printed in the USA
LVHW011253200821
695698LV00003B/304

9 780995 935426